GOODFOOD

SECRETS OF SUCCESS

BBC GOODFOOD

Secrets of Success

BBC Books

Please note that recipes containing raw eggs should not be served to babies, the elderly, the sick or pregnant women.

Front cover: Spiced seafood salad (page 33), Spiced pork with crackling (page 79) and Orange and lemon sorbets (page 166)

Back cover: Penne with prawns and sweetcorn (page 50). Rich chocolate cake (page 154) and Dinner rolls (page 129)

Published by BBC Books,
a division of BBC Enterprises Limited,
Woodlands, 80 Wood Lane
London W12 0TT

First published 1994
© BBC GOOD FOOD Magazine 1994

ISBN 0 563 37058 0
Jacket photograph by James Murphy
Home Economist Allyson Birch
Set in Helvetica by Selwood Systems, Midsomer Norton
Printed and bound in Great Britain by BPC Paulton Books Ltd, Paulton
Colour separation by Dot Gradations Ltd, Chelmsford
Jacket printed by Belmont Press Ltd, Northampton

Contents

Acknowledgments

BBC Good Food and BBC Books gratefully acknowledge the help of Joanna Farrow; Linda Fraser, Sarah Barrass, Sara Lewis, Mary Gwynn, Jacqueline Clark and Mary Cadogan, for the recipes they developed for the *Secrets of Success* series, and the following photographers, stylists and home economists.

Starters and Soups: photographers James Duncan, Steve Baxter, James Murphy and Struan Wallace, stylists Madeleine Brehaut, Maria Jacques, Andrea Lambton and Kay McGlone, home economists Sara Lewis, Jacqueline Clark and Louise Pickford, recipes Joanna Farrow and Petra Jackson;

Salads: photographers Gus Filgate, James Duncan and Graham Kirk, stylists Suzy Gittins, Madeleine Brehaut and Helen Payne, home economists Joanna Farrow and Jacqueline Clark;

Eggs: phtographer Gus Filgate, stylist Suzy Gittins, recipes and home economy Joanna Farrow;

Pasta: photographers Alan Newnham and Gus Filgate, stylists Maria Jacques and Helen Trent, recipes and home economy Linda Fraser, Sarah Barrass and Mary Cadogan, home economist Janet Smith;

Fish: photographers James Duncan, Struan Wallace, James Murphy and Steve Baxter, stylists Kay McGlone, Madeleine Brehaut, Andrea Lambton and Suzy Gittins, home economists Joanna Farrow, Linda Fraser, Jacqueline Clark and Meg Jansz;

Shellfish: photographer James Duncan, stylist Madeleine Brehaut, recipes and home economy Joanna Farrow;

Poultry: photographer James Duncan, stylist Madeleine Brehaut, recipes and home economy Joanna Farrow;

Meat: photographer James Duncan, stylist Madeleine Brehaut, recipes Joanna Farrow, home economist Sue Maggs;

Casseroles: photographers James Duncan, Jess Koppel and James Murphy, stylists Maria Jacques and Madeleine Brehaut, recipes and home economy Sara Lewis and Joanna Farrow, home economist Sue Maggs;

Pulses: photographer James Duncan, stylist Madeleine Brehaut, recipes and home economy Joanna Farrow;

Vegetables: photographer Ferguson Hill, Gus Filgate, Vernon Morgan and Struan Wallace, stylists Penny Makham, Maria Jacques, Suzy Gittins, Kay McGlone, recipes Orla Broderick and Louise Pickford, home economists Wendy Lee, Linda Tubby, Kathy Mann and Sarah Maxwell;

Batters: photographer James Duncan, stylist Madeleine Brehaut, recipes and home economy Joanna Farrow, home economist Sara Lewis;

Pastry: photographers James Duncan and Martin Brigdale, stylists Madeleine Brehaut and Andrea Lambton, recipes and home economy Joanna Farrow and Mary Gwynn, home economist Meg Jansz;

Bread: photographer James Duncan, stylist Madeleine Brehaut, recipes and home economy Joanna Farrow;

Biscuits: photographer Jess Koppel, recipes and home economy Linda Fraser and Sarah Barrass;

Cakes: photographer Steve Baxter, stylist Suzy Gittins, recipes and home economy Jacqueline Clark and Sarah Barrass;

Chocolate: photographers James Duncan and Jess Koppel, stylists Madeleine Brehaut and Andrea Lambton, recipes and home economy Linda Fraser, Sarah Barrass and Joanna Farrow;

Desserts: photographers James Duncan and Martin Brigdale, stylists Madeleine Brehaut and Andrea Lambton, recipes and home economy Joanna Farrow and Jacqueline Clark;

Preserves: photographers Struan Wallace and James Duncan, stylists Suzy Gittins and Madeleine Brehaut, recipes and home economy Joanna Farrow.

Introduction

Learn the secrets of successful cooking with *BBC Good Food* Magazine's very first book. Regular readers will remember *Secrets of Success*, our most popular monthly feature which ran for nearly three years, and will recognise many of the recipes. Now our friends at BBC Books have compiled the recipes, and added some new ones, to form a cookery bible that we know you'll want to keep handy in the kitchen.

Secrets of Success is a collection of basic cookery techniques combined with inspirational recipes for every occasion. Whether you're a beginner or a more experienced cook, the step-by-step sequences covering techniques such as filleting fish, making bread doughs, creating classic pâtés or making your own pasta will give you confidence to tackle the more elaborate dishes with ease. So when you next want to cook a simple cake for the kids or an elegant party gâteau, a quick chicken supper or a fabulous stuffed galantine for a wedding reception, a simple prawn starter or a stylish fish stew, *Secrets of Success* will show you how.

This book and indeed the magazine features would not have been possible without my very dedicated staff. Huge thanks go to the magazine's art director, Angela Dukes, for directing the food photography so beautifully, to Linda Fraser for writing many of the recipes and editing the series in the magazine, and to Becky Warren Smith for her meticulous sub-editing. Many of Joanna Farrow's recipes have been used for the book, providing us with delicious and beautiful dishes to photograph, and thanks also go to Sara Lewis, Jacqueline Clark and all the creative home economists who have worked on the *Secrets of Success* series. It is the skill and professionalism of the many superb food photographers, stylists and home economists which have helped to make *BBC Good Food* magazine so popular with our readers. *Secrets of Success* is the first of many books that I hope we publish, so my thanks also go to Charlotte Lochhead at BBC Books for her patience and dedication in translating magazine features into an accessible and friendly book and to Sara Kidd and Martin Hendry for putting together the jigsaw puzzle of pictures and layouts.

Most of all, a big thank you to our readers, many of whom have written or told me how much they have enjoyed the *Secrets of Success* recipes. This book is for you.

Happy cooking.

Mitzie

Mitzie Wilson
Editor-in-chief
BBC Good Food

Starters and Soups

*Soups, pâtés and tasty ideas that are deceptively
simple to make and look absolutely stunning
when served. Ideal as starters or light main meals.*

Seafood terrine

Serves 10

double quantity Basic fish pâté purée (see steps 1–4 overleaf) without the herbs

225g/8oz peeled prawns

1 tbsp tomato purée

4 tbsp chopped fresh dill or parsley

225g/8 oz smoked haddock or cod fillet

fresh herbs, to garnish

❶ Mix half the fish purée with half the prawns and the tomato purée and blend until smooth. Stir the remaining prawns and the herbs into the rest of the fish purée.

❷ Butter a deep, 1.25 litre/$2\frac{1}{2}$ pint ring mould. Spoon the tomato mixture into the mould and spread up sides to leave a trough in centre.

❸ Spoon half of the herb mixture into trough. Thinly slice smoked fish and arrange over filling. Cover with remaining herb mixture and smooth surface over.

❹ Cover mould with foil and place in roasting tin with 1cm/$\frac{1}{2}$ inch depth boiling water. Bake at 190C/375F/Gas 5 for 1 hour 15 minutes until just firm. Leave in tin for 10 minutes, then loosen edges of mould and turn out onto flat plate. Serve garnished with fresh herbs.

From left: Chequered salmon wraps (recipe overleaf) and Seafood terrine

BASIC FISH PÂTÉ

Virtually any fish can be used for a light, moussey pâté that's delicious warm or cold. This basic sole and herb pâté recipe can be flavoured with different herbs, or pieces of smoked fish. Layering contrasting purées also looks effective.

Serves 6

450g/1lb sole or any other white fish

2 eggs

150ml/$\frac{1}{4}$ pt double cream

2–3 tbsp chopped fresh herbs (parsley, dill, fennel, chives)

$\frac{1}{4}$ tsp salt

❶ Skin the fish by moving a knife in a sawing motion between the skin and flesh. Carefully pull out any remaining bones, then chop flesh coarsely.

❷ Tip the chopped fish (in batches if necessary) into a food processor or blender.

Chequered salmon wraps

Serves 12

1 quantity Basic fish pâté purée (see steps 1–4 above) made with huss and omitting herbs

1 tsp tomato purée

1 quantity Basic fish pâté purée (see steps 1–4 above)

225g/8oz smoked salmon trout

chives, to garnish

❶ Mix huss purée with tomato purée and spread into a greaseproof-lined shallow 15 cm/7 inch square tin. Spread basic fish purée over top.

❷ Cover with foil and place in a roasting tin with 1cm/$\frac{1}{2}$ inch boiling water. Bake at 190C/375F/Gas 5 for about 50 minutes until just firm. Cool.

❸ Turn out pâté and peel off paper. Cut pâté into 1cm/$\frac{1}{2}$ inch strips then press 2 strips together inverting one to give chequered effect. Repeat with rest of pâté.

❹ Cover top and sides of each chequered strip with smoked salmon trout, trimming and

overlapping to fit.

❺ Cut each strip into three lengths. Wrap each piece with a chive, tying with a small knot. Trim off ends.

Mackerel and lime pâté

Serves 4–6

2 × 150g/5oz cans mackerel in oil

200g/7oz medium–fat cream cheese

grated rind of 1 lime

seasoning

toasted Granary bread, to serve

❶ Place the mackerel in a food processor with the cream cheese, lime rind and seasoning, then blend until smooth. Or place the ingredients in a bowl and beat together until smooth. Serve with toast.

Smoked haddock with avocado, lime and chilli

This dressing pickles the fish so that it can be served as a raw piquant salad.

Serves 6

450g/1lb smoked haddock, very thinly sliced

1 avocado

FOR THE DRESSING

150ml/$\frac{1}{4}$ pint olive oil

3 tbsp lime juice

2 red chillies, finely sliced

seasoning

❶ Lay the haddock in a china or glass dish. Mix the dressing ingredients, pour over the fish, and leave in a cool place for several hours.

❷ Halve, peel, stone and slice the avocado. Lay the avocado on top of the fish and spoon over the dressing in the dish. Serve with a green salad.

❸ If you don't have a processor or blender, fish can be finely chopped and then mashed by hand before beating in the eggs, cream, herbs and seasoning.

❹ Add the eggs to the food processor and whizz until the mixture is a smooth purée. Preheat oven to 190C/375F/Gas 5.

❺ Turn into a buttered terrine. Cover with foil, place in roasting tin with 1cm/½ inch boiling water. Bake for 45 minutes. Allow to cool. Turn out and decorate with herbs. Serve sliced with toast.

Layered fish terrine

Serves 6–8

oil, for greasing
2 large lemon sole, filleted
5 large trout fillets
200g/7oz medium–fat soft cheese
175g/6oz Greek strained yogurt
2 tbsp double cream
75g/3 oz watercress
1 egg
freshly grated nutmeg
seasoning

❶ Preheat the oven to 190C/375F/Gas 5. Grease a 1kg/2lb terrine or loaf tin with oil.
❷ Skin the sole and trout fillets. Place single layers of fish between two sheets of damp greaseproof paper and beat lightly with a rolling pin to flatten. Use the sole to line the base of the tin, cutting fillets to fit, and reserve enough to cover the top.
❸ Blend together the cheese, yogurt, cream, watercress and egg in a food processor. Season well and add nutmeg.
❹ Prop the terrine or loaf tin

against a thick board so it is tilted at an angle of 45°. Spoon a layer of cheese mixture into the bottom end and cover with a strip of trout, cut to fit. Repeat layers to make a diagonal pattern and cover with the reserved sole.
❺ Stand the terrine upright in a roasting tin filled to a 1cm/½in depth with boiling water. Cover with foil and bake for 35–40 minutes until the fish feels firm when pierced with a knife. Leave to cool in the tin, then serve cut into slices.

Grilled sardines

Fresh sardines also taste delicious when barbecued. Gut sardines if you prefer a more delicate taste.

Serves 4

675g/1½ lb fresh sardines
2 tbsp coarse sea salt
small handful fresh herbs, such as rosemary, thyme, oregano and marjoram, chopped

❶ Run a knife against the skin of the sardines to remove scales. Gut the fish or leave them whole, then wash and dry on kitchen paper. Slash each one several times on both sides.
❷ Sprinkle sardines with the salt and tuck the herbs into the cavities (if you're leaving the fish whole, sprinkle the herbs on top). Allow to stand for 30 minutes.
❸ Grill the sardines for 1½–2 minutes on each side until the skins turn crisp.

BASIC VEGETABLE PURÉE

Creamy vegetable purées are a lighter alternative to traditional pâtés. Most vegetables that purée easily work well, and can be enhanced with herbs and spices.

Serves 6

450g/1lb broccoli, cauliflower, carrots, celeriac or asparagus

4 eggs

300ml/$\frac{1}{2}$ pt double cream

$\frac{1}{4}$ tsp grated nutmeg

seasoning

❶ Trim and roughly chop chosen vegetable and place in a steamer over a pan of hot water. Bring to the boil and steam for 15–20 minutes until tender, depending on vegetable. Or boil in a little water.

❷ Thoroughly drain vegetable and transfer to a food processor or blender. (If using a blender you'll need to purée half the quantity at a time.)

Triple vegetable terrine

For added flavour use clear vegetable stock or a splash of white wine with the water when making gelatine layer. Quail's eggs can be used instead of the egg. Store terrines for up to 2 days.

Serves 10

half quantity each of broccoli, cauliflower and carrot purées (see Basic vegetable purée steps 1–4 above)

3 tsp gelatine

225g/8 oz cream cheese

seasoning

FOR THE GARNISH

several baby corn cobs

1 egg, hard-boiled

several baby carrots

❶ Spoon broccoli purée into a greased 1.75 litre/3 pint terrine or ovenproof dish. Carefully spoon cauliflower purée over broccoli then top with carrot purée.

❷ Preheat oven to 160C/325F/ Gas 3. Cover terrine with foil and stand dish in a roasting tin. Add 1 cm/$\frac{1}{2}$ inch depth water and bake for about 1 hour 15 minutes until firm to the touch. Cool completely.

❸ Sprinkle gelatine over 4 tbsp water and leave for 5 minutes. Add to 300ml/$\frac{1}{2}$ pint boiling water and stir until dissolved. Cool.

❹ Beat half gelatine with cream cheese and seasoning, and pour over terrine. Chill until set.

❺ Blanch baby corn cobs and carrots in boiling water for 1 minute. Slice the egg and use with the corn and baby carrots to decorate terrine. Spoon remaining gelatine over top and chill until set.

❸ Add the eggs to the vegetable and purée until the mixture is completely smooth, scraping up any pieces of vegetable from the side of the bowl.

❹ Stir in the cream and nutmeg until evenly combined. Season generously. Grease 6 individual ramekins or 1 large ovenproof dish. Preheat oven to 180C/350F/ Gas 4.

❺ Turn mixture into ramekins or dish. Place in a roasting tin and pour in 1cm/$\frac{1}{2}$ inch depth boiling water. Cover with foil and bake for 30 minutes for ramekins, 50 minutes for dish. Allow to cool. Serve with salad.

Spicy cauliflower parcels

Serves 6

$\frac{1}{2}$ tsp coriander seeds

$\frac{1}{2}$ tsp cumin seeds

1 tbsp fennel seeds

1 quantity cauliflower purée (see Basic vegetable purée, steps 1–4 above)

$\frac{1}{4}$ tsp dries crushed chillies

$\frac{1}{4}$ tsp ground turmeric

$\frac{1}{2}$ tbsp chopped fresh coriander or parsley

100g/4 oz fresh spinach leaves

cherry tomatoes, avocado slices and parsley or chervil, to garnish

❶ Lightly butter 6 ramekin dishes.
❷ Crush seeds with a pestle and mortar or in a bowl with the end of a rolling pin. Add to cauliflower purée with chillies, turmeric and coriander or parsley.
❸ Remove stalks from spinach. Bring a large pan of water to the boil. Remove from heat. Add spinach leaves, a handful at a time, and leave for about 10 seconds until softened. Drain. Use spinach leaves to line dishes.

❹ Spoon cauliflower purée into dishes. Bring ends of spinach leaves over purée. Place dishes in a roasting tin and cook as in step 5 above. Leave in dishes for 10 minutes then invert on to plate. Garnish with tomatoes, avocado and herbs.

From left: Triple vegetable terrine and Spicy cauliflower parcels

BASIC MEAT PÂTÉ

A classic pâté combines meats, liver and plenty of spices. Coarse or smooth, pork and rabbit pâté makes a tasty lunch dish.

Serves 8–10

225g/8 oz pig's liver

450g/1lb skinned and boned belly pork

350g/12 oz diced rabbit or lean pork

3 garlic cloves, peeled

$\frac{1}{4}$ tsp ground nutmeg

$\frac{1}{4}$ ground allspice

3 tbsp brandy

seasoning

❶ Roughly chop the pig's liver. Using a sharp knife, cut the belly pork into strips, then across into chunks. Combine with the diced rabbit or lean pork.

❷ Put half the meats and the garlic in a food processor and whizz quickly for a chunky pâté, or longer for a smoother consistency. Process remaining mixture.

Pâté en croûte

Serves 10

75g/3 oz pistachio nuts, shelled

1 quantity Basic meat pâté (see steps 1–3 above)

350g/12 oz shortcrust pastry

egg yolk, to glaze

sprigs of parsley, to garnish

❶ Beat pistachio nuts into uncooked pâté mixture. Pack into a 900g/2lb loaf tin and bake as in step 4 above. Press pâté with weights and leave to cool completely.

❷ Turn out the pâté and scrape off any jellied stock.

❸ Roll out pastry on a floured surface to a rectangle large enough to cover pâté. Position pâté, narrow side down, on pastry. Cut corners off pastry, then bring sides up over pâté to cover

completely. Pinch edges together, then place seam side down on a baking sheet and brush with egg yolk.

❹ Preheat oven to 200C/400F/Gas 6. Re-roll pastry trimmings and use to decorate pâté. Brush with egg yolk.

❺ Bake pâté for 25 minutes or until pastry is golden. Cool, garnish with parsley and serve sliced.

From left: Pâté en croûte and Latticed liver and mushroom pâté

3 Transfer mixture to a large bowl and stir in the spices, brandy and seasoning. Turn mixture into a 900g/2lb loaf tin. Preheat oven to 160C/325F/Gas 3.

4 Stand container in a roasting tin. Cover pâté with foil. Pour 1cm/$\frac{1}{2}$ inch water into tin and bake for 1$\frac{1}{2}$ hours or until juices run clear when a knife is inserted.

5 Leave to cool slightly, then cover pâté with a plate or foil-covered card and weight down with kitchen scale weights or food cans. Too much weight can press out all the juices. 750g/$\frac{1}{2}$lb is about right. Refrigerate when completely cool.

Latticed liver and mushroom pâté

Serves 10

75ml/3 fl oz white wine

100g/4 oz button mushrooms, sliced

1 quantity Basic meat pâté (see steps 1–3 above), substituting 450g/1lb chicken livers for the rabbit or lean pork, and processing finely

4 rashers streaky bacon, rind removed

strip of pork fat

1 tbsp gelatine

1 Beat the wine and mushrooms into uncooked pâté mixture and turn into a 1.5 litre/2$\frac{1}{2}$ pint terrine. Bake as steps 3 and 4 above allowing an extra 15 minutes cooking, but . . .

2 Half way through cooking remove pâté from oven. Stretch and halve bacon rashers lengthways. Cut pork fat into thin strips. Lay rashers across pâté then lattice with the pork strips. Tuck ends down sides of pâté and complete cooking.

3 Drain off juices, reserving 2 tablespoons. Weight down pâté and leave to cool.

4 Sprinkle gelatine over 4 tbsp water and leave for 5 minutes. Bring 300ml/$\frac{1}{2}$ pint water to the boil and add reserved juices. Stir until dissolved.

5 Pour over pâté and leave to set.

Chicken and pork terrine

Serves 8–10

1 quantity of finely minced Basic meat pâté (see page 14, steps 1–3)

50g/2 oz streaky bacon

1 small red pepper

1 small yellow pepper

1 large boneless chicken breast

100g/4 oz French beans

1 tbsp gelatine

❶ Make a finely minced Basic meat pâté, (see page 14, steps 1–3), but add the streaky bacon during step 2. Spoon a 0.5 cm/$\frac{1}{4}$ in layer into a 900g/2 lb loaf tin.

❷ Thinly slice the red and yellow peppers. Cut each slice and open out into a strip. Cut the chicken breast lengthways into 4. Top and tail the French beans.

❸ Preheat oven to 160C/325F/ Gas 3.

❹ Arrange a line of chicken breast lengthways over the pâté and surround with beans. Continue to build up pâté adding strips of pepper lengthways and another layer of pâté, chicken and beans. Bake as in Basic meat pâté, step 4 page 15 and press as in step 5.

❺ Drain excess juice, reserving 2 tablespoons. Sprinkle gelatine over 4 tablespoons of water and leave for 5 minutes. Bring 300 ml/ $\frac{1}{2}$ pint water to the boil and add gelatine and reserved juices. Stir until dissolved and pour around pâté while still in tin.

❻ Leave to set.

❼ Dip tin briefly in boiling water before turning out.

Below: Chicken and pork terrine

Melba toast

Toast medium sliced bread on both sides. Using a sharp knife cut through centre of toast to give wafer thin layers. Cut into small squares. Grill untoasted side for about 1 minute until beginning to curl.

Citrus twists

Pare a long strip of skin from an orange, lemon and lime. Cut away remaining skin and thinly slice flesh. Finely slice pared skin. Make a knot from one shred and thread more shreds through it. Arrange over citrus slices.

Radish chrysanthemums

Trim ends from radish. Make close cuts, almost through to stalk. Turn radish and make cuts in opposite direction. Place in a bowl of cold water and leave until radish has opened out.

Spring onion tassels

Cut 5 cm/2 in lengths from white ends of spring onions. Make lengthways cuts, half way up onion, rotating as you cut. Leave in cold water for at least 30 minutes until ends curl.

Tomato roses

Using a potato peeler, peel a long strip of skin from a large tomato (like peeling an apple). Roll up strip loosely to make a small rose. Use tomato roses with sprigs of mint or leafy herbs to garnish pâté.

Chunky fish soup with rouille

You should serve the rouille paste in a separate bowl on the table so everyone can add a little to the soup. But be careful – it's pretty hot stuff.

Serves 6

FOR THE ROUILLE

1 red pepper, seeded and chopped
3 garlic cloves, peeled
1 tsp hot chilli powder
25g/1oz fresh breadcrumbs
4 tbsp olive oil

FOR THE SOUP

1 tsp saffron strands
225g/8oz monkfish
450g/1lb cod or haddock fillet
2 small snapper or red mullet
225g/8oz mussels or clams, scrubbed
2 large onions, sliced
3 celery sticks, sliced
2 tbsp olive oil
2 pared strips orange rind
1 tbsp plain flour
900ml/1½ pints fish stock
675g/1½lb new potatoes, scrubbed
2 tbsp chopped fresh herbs, such as chives, dill and tarragon
4 tbsp double cream
seasoning

❶ To make the rouille, blend the pepper, garlic, chilli powder and breadcrumbs in a food processor. Gradually whizz in the oil and transfer to a small bowl. Set aside.
❷ Pour 1 tablespoon of boiling water over the saffron and set aside. Remove the cartilage from monkfish and cut flesh into chunks. Skin cod or haddock, removing bones, and cut into large pieces. Clean snapper or mullet, scrape away the scales with a sharp knife and remove the heads. Cut into pieces. Discard any damaged mussels or clams and those that remain open when tapped.
❸ Fry the onions and celery in the oil. Add orange rind and flour, then stir in the stock and saffron. Add the potatoes and a pinch of salt and bring to the boil. Simmer until tender, then stir in the fresh herbs.
❹ Lay fish (except mussels or clams) in the pan, cover and simmer for 10 minutes. Add shellfish, cover and cook for 3 minutes until they open. Discard any that remain closed. Stir in the cream and season.

Left: Chunky fish soup with rouille

Carrot and ginger soup with fragrant lemon oil

This tasty, sweet-and-sour soup is given an extra special touch with the addition of a crispy ginger and lemon garnish and tangy lemon oil.

Serves 4–6

25g/1oz butter

1 onion, chopped

1 garlic clove, chopped

2 tsp grated fresh root ginger

675g/1½lb carrots, scrubbed and chopped

1 tsp chopped fresh thyme

grated rind and juice of ½ lemon

900ml/1½ pints vegetable stock

150ml/¼ pint single cream

seasoning

FOR THE GARNISH

4 tbsp olive oil

4 strips lemon rind, finely shredded

1 baby onion, thinly sliced

2 slices fresh root ginger, finely shredded

few fresh thyme leaves

1 tbsp lemon juice

lemon oil (from delicatessens)

❶ Melt the butter in a large pan. Add the chopped onion and garlic, grated ginger, carrots, chopped thyme and grated lemon rind and sauté together for 10 minutes. Add the lemon juice and stock and bring to the boil, then cover and simmer gently for 25 minutes.

❷ Prepare the garnish, heat 1 tablespoon of the oil in a frying pan. Add the lemon rind, onion, ginger and thyme leaves and stir fry for 2–3 minutes until everything is crisp and golden. Drain thoroughly on kitchen paper. Add remaining oil to the pan and whisk in the lemon juice. Set aside.

❸ When the soup has finished simmering, purée it until it is quite smooth. Add the cream and seasoning to taste, then heat the soup through without allowing it to boil. Serve topped with the crispy garnish mixture and a drizzle of lemon oil.

Watercress soup

Serves 6

50g/2oz butter

1 onion, thinly sliced

225g/8oz potatoes, diced

3 bunches watercress, trimmed

1 tsp salt

1 tsp golden caster sugar

¼ tsp ground mace

900ml/1½ pints chicken stock

150ml/¼ pint double cream

seasoning

croûtons, to garnish

❶ Melt the butter in a heavy-based pan and fry the onion for 5 minutes or until softened. Add the potatoes, watercress, salt, sugar, mace and stock to the pan and stir over a gentle heat until boiling.

❷ Reduce the heat, cover the pan and simmer for 20 minutes or until the potatoes are tender.

❸ Liquidise in two batches until smooth. Return the soup to a pan, stir in half of the cream with seasoning to taste and reheat gently. Top with a swirl of cream and garnish with the croûtons.

Below: Carrot and ginger soup with fragrant lemon oil

Smoked haddock and corn chowder

Serves 6

450g/1 lb smoked haddock fillet, skinned and boned

150ml/$\frac{1}{4}$ pint milk

2 tbsp olive oil

2 leeks, trimmed and sliced

1 small red pepper, seeded and diced

225g/8oz potatoes, roughly chopped

200g/7oz can sweetcorn, drained

1.2 litres/2 pints fish stock

6 fresh parsley stalks, chopped

1 tsp lemon juice

seasoning

❶ Place the smoked haddock in a large, heavy-based pan and pour over the milk. Cover and simmer for 6–8 minutes or until the fish flakes easily. Drain, reserve liquid and allow fish to cool a little.

❷ Heat the oil in the pan and fry the leeks and pepper for 2–3 minutes or until tender, but not coloured. Add the potatoes, sweetcorn, reserved cooking liquid and stock and bring to boil. Cover and simmer for about 15 minutes or until the potatoes are tender.

❸ Meanwhile, flake the fish, remove any skin and bones and stir the flesh into the soup. Add the parsley, lemon juice and seasoning and heat through.

Goulash soup

Serves 6

2 tbsp olive oil

350g/12oz lean braising steak, cut into bite-sized cubes

1 large onion, thinly sliced

1 garlic clove, crushed

1 tbsp sweet paprika

1 tbsp plain flour

400g/14oz can tomatoes

2 tbsp tomato purée

1.2 litres/2 pints beef stock

$\frac{1}{2}$ tsp caraway seeds

pinch of sugar

1 large potato, diced

150ml/$\frac{1}{4}$ pint soured cream

3 tsp snipped fresh chives and paprika, to garnish

❶ Heat the oil in a large, heavy-based pan. Add the meat and brown over a medium heat, then remove with a slotted spoon.

❷ Add the onion and garlic to the pan and fry for 5 minutes or until golden. Reduce the heat, add the paprika and flour and cook, stirring for 1 minute.

❸ Remove the pan from the heat and gradually stir in the tomatoes, tomato purée and stock, then add the meat, caraway seeds and sugar.

❹ Bring the soup to the boil, stirring constantly. Cover the pan and simmer, stirring occasionally, for 1 hour or until the meat is tender. Add the potato and cook for 15 minutes.

❺ Serve the soup topped with a swirl of soured cream and garnish with a sprinkling of snipped chives and paprika.

From top left clockwise: Smoked haddock and corn chowder, Goulash soup and Country bean soup

Country bean soup

Serves 6

75g/3oz dried butter beans, soaked for 6 hours or overnight

75g/3oz dried black-eyed beans, soaked for 6 hours or overnight

2 tbsp olive oil

1 medium onion, thinly sliced

4 small leeks, trimmed and sliced

2 large carrots, scrubbed and sliced

2 celery sticks, sliced

100g/4oz swede, roughly chopped

225g/8oz chorizo sausage, thickly sliced

2 × 400g/14oz cans chopped tomatoes

1–2 tbsp tomato purée

1.5 litres/2½ pints chicken stock

50g/2oz soup pasta

FOR THE PISTOU

25g/1oz fresh basil leaves

2 garlic cloves, peeled

6 tbsp olive oil

50g/2oz Gruyère, finely grated

seasoning

crusty bread, to serve

❶ Drain the butter beans and black-eyed beans, place in two separate pans and cover with water. Bring to the boil and boil fast for 10 minutes, then simmer for 1½ hours or until tender. Drain and set aside.

❷ Heat the olive oil in a large, heavy-based pan. Add the onion, leeks, carrots, celery, swede and chorizo and gently fry for 5 minutes or until tender, but not browned.

❸ Stir in the reserved beans, tomatoes, tomato purée, stock and soup pasta. Bring to the boil, reduce the heat, cover and simmer gently for about 30 minutes or until the vegetables are just cooked.

❹ Meanwhile, make the pistou: place the basil leaves, garlic, olive oil and Gruyère in a food processor and whizz until the mixture is well blended. Season to taste.

❺ Stir a little of the pistou into each bowl of soup and pass round the remainder in a small bowl. Serve with crusty bread.

Cream of leek soup

Serves 4

50g/2oz butter

1 onion, finely chopped

450g/1lb leeks, finely chopped

1 carrot, finely chopped

300ml/½ pint milk

900ml/1½ pints chicken or vegetable stock

seasoning

a little lemon juice (optional)

4 tbsp single cream (optional) and sprigs of tarragon, to garnish

❶ Melt the butter and gently fry the onion for 5 minutes, then add leeks and carrot. Cook for 10–15 minutes until soft, stirring occasionally.

❷ Add milk and stock and bring to the boil. Cover and simmer for 25 minutes. Leave to cool. Liquidise until smooth. Strain through sieve.

❸ To serve, return the soup to the pan and reheat gently. Season, adding a little lemon juice, if desired, to sharpen the flavour. Garnish each bowl with single cream, and a tarragon sprig.

Lemony butter bean soup

Serves 2–3

15g/½oz butter or margarine

400g/14oz can butter beans, drained and rinsed

1 garlic clove, crushed

juice and finely grated rind of 1 lemon

750ml/1¼ pints vegetable stock

1 tbsp chopped fresh parsley

2 tbsp single cream

seasoning

❶ Melt the butter or margarine in a medium-sized pan, then add the beans, garlic, lemon juice and rind. Cook over a gentle heat for 5–7 minutes, stirring frequently.

❷ Add the vegetable stock to the bean mixture and gradually bring to the boil. Cover the soup, reduce the heat and simmer for 5 minutes.

❸ Process the soup until smooth. Return to a clean pan and stir in the chopped parsley and cream. Season to taste and gently reheat, but do not boil. Serve hot with bread topped with toasted goat's cheese to serve.

Below: Lemony butter bean soup

Salads

Stylish, original and healthy, salads are so versatile, and easy to create and prepare. They are also really practical for transporting to barbecues and picnics.

Classic vinaigrette

❶ Mix 4 tablespoons of wine vinegar, 1 teaspoon of Dijon mustard and 150ml/¼pint of oil in a screw-topped jar and shake thoroughly. Season to taste; if too sharp, add a little oil or a pinch of sugar. If too oily add a little vinegar. Store in a screw top jar.

Oil options

Vinaigrette dressings are mainly oil-based, so be careful in your choice of oil. There are all sorts available – simply vary the flavour to suit the salad.

Olive oil goes well with Mediterranean-style vegetables and herbs. Nutty oils complement bitter leaves, such as frisée and chicory. Sunflower or grapeseed oils can be used together with more strongly flavoured oils.

Vary the vinegar

Well-flavoured vinegars are essential for salad dressings. Do not use malt vinegar or distilled white vinegar – these are made from sour, unhopped beer and are far too strong in flavour.

Balsamic vinegar

Comes only from the Modena area in northern Italy. Dark and mellow with a wonderfully sweet-and-sour flavour. Don't mask the taste with any pungent ingredients (e.g. garlic or mustard). Very expensive, but a little goes a long way.

Wine vinegars

Made from both red and white wines, work well with added flavourings. On the other hand, sherry vinegar has a lovely, full, rounded flavour and is best on its own.

Fruit vinegars

Now widely available. Make your own by steeping fresh fruit in wine vinegar, then strain it. Raspberry vinegar is probably the most well known and it complements dark, rich meats like duck.

Cider vinegar

Differs in that it is made from fermented vinegar. Its strong, appley flavour makes a pleasant dressing.

Rice wine vinegar

Is produced in both China and Japan. Chinese is quite sharp and sour while Japanese has a much mellower, almost sweet flavour and it makes a good vinaigrette with nut oil.

From left: Potato and beetroot salad, Grilled summer salad, mixed green salad, French bean and beefsteak tomato salad and Shredded vegetable salad (recipes overleaf)

Shredded vegetable salad

Serves 4 as a side salad
1 large courgette
$\frac{1}{2}$ medium mooli (Japanese radish)
1 large carrot
$\frac{1}{2}$ small head of Chinese leaves, finely shredded
3 tbsp mayonnaise
3 tbsp Classic vinaigrette (see page 23)
2 tbsp snipped fresh chives

❶ Cut the courgette, mooli and carrot into very thin julienne, about 10cm/4in long. Place in a salad bowl with the Chinese leaves.
❷ Mix together the mayonnaise and vinaigrette and pour over the salad. Scatter in the chives and toss lightly to combine. Serve chilled.

Grilled summer salad

Serves 4 as a side salad
225g/8oz shiitake mushrooms
1 small aubergine, thickly sliced
1 red, 1 yellow, 1 green pepper, seeded and cut into large chunks
few fresh sprigs of thyme
4–6 tbsp extra virgin olive oil
FOR THE DRESSING
2 tbsp balsamic vinegar
6 tbsp extra virgin olive oil
2 tbsp chopped fresh thyme
seasoning

❶ Arrange the vegetables on a grill rack, tuck the thyme around them and brush with oil. Grill for 5 minutes, turning and basting with oil, until tender and golden.
❷ Meanwhile, mix dressing ingredients. Transfer hot vegetables to a dish. Pour over cooking juices and dressing. Serve warm.

French bean and beefsteak tomato salad

Serves 6 as a side salad
225g/8oz French beans, trimmed
3 beefsteak tomatoes, sliced
FOR THE DRESSING
3tbsp wine vinegar
150ml/$\frac{1}{4}$ pint extra virgin olive oil
1 tsp tarragon mustard, or 1 tsp mild mustard and 1 tsp chopped fresh tarragon
handful of fresh parsley, chopped
seasoning

❶ Place the French beans in a pan of boiling, salted water. Cover and cook for 3–5 minutes until almost tender – they should still be quite crisp when ready. Drain and refresh the beans under cold water and set aside.
❷ Arrange the beans and tomato slices on a large platter. Mix together the dressing ingredients and pour over the vegetables. Leave the salad to marinate at room temperature for about 30 minutes, then serve.

Potato and beetroot salad

There are several varieties of waxy salad potatoes that are at their best when served cold. If they are unavailable, use small new potatoes instead.

Serves 4 as a side salad
675g/1$\frac{1}{2}$ lb waxy potatoes
4 tbsp extra virgin olive oil
1 tbsp cumin seeds
600g/1$\frac{1}{4}$ lb cooked beetroot, cut into 5mm/$\frac{1}{4}$ in thick sticks
3 tbsp Classic vinaigrette (see page 23)
2 tbsp snipped fresh dill
seasoning

❶ Cook the potatoes in boiling, salted water for 15–20 minutes until tender. Drain and cut into thick slices.
❷ Heat the oil in a pan, add the cumin seeds and cook for a minute or two until they begin to pop. Remove from the heat, add the potatoes and toss to coat in the oil. Set aside to cool.
❸ Mix the beetroot with the vinaigrette and spoon into the centre of a dish. Arrange potatoes around edge. Scatter dill on top and season. Serve at room temperature.

Baby carrot and sweetcorn salad

Baby vegetables are delicate, delicious and full of flavour. There's no need to peel or scrape the carrots – trim the tops, leaving about 1cm/$\frac{1}{2}$in. Don't throw away the frondy leaves – they're edible and very pretty.

Serves 4 as a side salad
225g/8oz baby carrots, trimmed
225g/8oz baby sweetcorn
FOR THE DRESSING
6 tbsp Greek strained yogurt
2 tsp chopped fresh mint
seasoning
50g/2oz flaked almonds, toasted, to serve

❶ Cook the baby carrots and sweetcorn in boiling water for about 2–3 minutes until tender but still crisp. Refresh them under cold water and then drain well in a colander. Arrange on a serving plate.
❷ Make the dressing by mixing together the yogurt, fresh mint and seasoning. Spoon over the salad, sprinkle with the flaked almonds and serve at once.

Lemony asparagus with Parmesan

Serves 4–6 as a starter

450g/1lb thin asparagus spears

50g/2oz piece Parmesan

FOR THE DRESSING

2–3 tbsp lemon juice

150ml/$\frac{1}{4}$ pint extra virgin olive oil

seasoning

❶ Cook the asparagus in boiling, salted water in an asparagus steamer, or lying flat in a large frying pan, for 3–5 minutes. Drain and refresh in cold water so as to cool quickly, then drain again and divide equally and arrange on serving plates.

❷ Mix the lemon juice, oil and seasoning and pour over the asparagus. Pare off curls of Parmesan with a vegetable peeler and scatter over. Serve at once.

Chilli chicken with cashew nuts

Serves 4 as a main course

225g/8oz brown long grain rice

1 tbsp sesame oil

75g/3oz cashew nuts

100g/4oz sugar-snap peas

2 cooked chicken breasts, sliced

1 mango, peeled, stoned and sliced

FOR THE DRESSING

3 tbsp sesame oil

6$\frac{1}{2}$tbsp sunflower oil

3 tbsp rice wine vinegar

seasoning

1 tbsp shredded fresh mint

1 tsp grated fresh root ginger

1 each fresh red, orange and green chillies, thinly sliced

❶ Cook the rice in boiling salted water for 30–35 minutes until just tender. Drain and leave to cool.

❷ Heat the sesame oil in a small frying pan and fry the cashew nuts until golden, then set aside. Cook the peas in a small pan of boiling, salted water for 2–3 minutes until just tender. Drain and rinse in cold water until cool.

❸ Place the cooked rice, cashew nuts, peas, sliced chicken and mango in a large bowl. Make the dressing by mixing together the oils, vinegar and seasoning, then stir in the mint, ginger and chillies. Pour the dressing over the salad and toss lightly. Chill until ready to serve.

Below: Lemony asparagus with Parmesan

Pasta salad with tuna and basil

If you are in a hurry, canned tuna steak can be used instead of fresh tuna – just drain it and flake into the pasta.

Serves 4 as a main course
225–350g/8–12oz penne (pasta quills)
75g/3oz black olives, drained
50g/2oz sun-dried tomatoes in oil, drained and chopped
4 tbsp extra virgin olive oil
4 tuna steaks, about 175g/6oz each
seasoning
FOR THE DRESSING
2 tbsp balsamic vinegar
2 tbsp walnut oil
4 tbsp extra virgin olive oil
10 fresh basil leaves, chopped
2 tbsp grated Parmesan
seasoning

❶ Make the dressing by mixing together the vinegar, oils, basil leaves, Parmesan and seasoning.
❷ Cook the pasta in plenty of boiling, salted water until *al dente*. Drain and rinse in cold water, then tip into a large bowl. Stir in the dressing, olives and sun-dried tomatoes.
❸ Heat the oil in a frying pan and add the tuna steaks. Season and fry over a medium heat for about 10 minutes until the tuna is golden brown on both sides and just cooked through (test with the point of a sharp knife). Serve at once with the pasta salad.

Roast beef and rocket

Serves 4 as a main course
450g/1lb fillet of beef
few handfuls of rocket
2 tbsp capers, drained
FOR THE DRESSING
2 tbsp red wine vinegar
6 tbsp extra virgin olive oil
1 tbsp wholegrain mustard
seasoning

❶ Preheat the oven to 200C/ 400F/Gas 6. Tie the beef into a neat shape with string, place on a rack in a roasting tin and cook for 20 minutes. Cool completely, slice thinly and arrange with the rocket.
❷ Make the dressing by mixing the vinegar, oil, mustard and seasoning. Add the capers and pour over the salad. Leave at room temperature for about 30 minutes before serving.

Ham and bean salad

Serves 4 as a main course
225g/8oz broad beans
400g/14oz can flageolet beans, drained
handful of oak leaf lettuce leaves
4 tbsp chopped fresh parsley
4 thick slices cooked ham
FOR THE DRESSING
2 tbsp white wine vinegar
6 tbsp extra virgin olive oil
1 tbsp clear honey
1 tbsp wholegrain mustard
1 garlic clove, crushed
seasoning

❶ Cook the broad beans in boiling, salted water for 4–5 minutes until just tender. Drain and rinse in cold water. Tip into a large bowl and mix in the flageolet beans, lettuce and parsley.
❷ Arrange the ham on a serving plate and spoon the bean salad around it. Make the dressing by mixing together the vinegar, oil, honey, mustard, garlic and seasoning. Spoon the dressing over the beans and ham. Chill until ready to serve.

Wild rice, bulgar wheat and trout salad

Serves 4 as a main course

175g/6oz bulgar wheat

100g/4oz wild rice

2 trout fillets, 75g/3oz each

1 tbsp extra virgin olive oil

4 tbsp snipped fresh chives

175g/6oz red and yellow cherry tomatoes, halved

FOR THE DRESSING

100ml/3½fl oz Classic vinaigrette (see page 23)

4 tbsp Greek strained yogurt

seasoning

❶ Place the bulgar wheat in a bowl with 900ml/1½ pints boiling water. Leave to soak and swell for 30 minutes, then drain. Cook the wild rice in boiling, salted water for about 35 minutes until just tender and then drain and leave to cool.

❷ Brush the trout fillets with the olive oil and season. Place, skin side down, on a rack, and grill for about 5 minutes until the flesh flakes easily. Leave to cool, then remove the skin and any bones, and break fish into large flakes.

❸ Put the trout into a large bowl with the bulgar wheat, rice, chives, and cherry tomatoes. Mix together the vinaigrette and yogurt, and season with plenty of ground black pepper. Pour the dressing over the salad and toss together lightly. Chill until ready to serve.

From left clockwise: Pasta salad with tuna and basil, Ham and bean salad and Wild rice, bulgar wheat and trout salad

Date, orange and radicchio salad

Serves 4 as a starter

2 oranges

225g/8oz fresh dates, halved and stoned

1 handful each radicchio and frisée leaves

FOR THE DRESSING

3 tbsp balsamic vinegar

3 tbsp extra virgin olive oil

3 tbsp walnut oil

seasoning

❶ Remove the peel and pith from the oranges, then divide into segments, holding the fruit over a bowl to catch the juice. Reserve juice and cut segments in half. Place in a salad bowl with the dates. Tear the radicchio and frisée into small pieces and mix into the fruit.

❷ Mix the vinegar, oils and seasoning into the reserved orange juice and pour over the salad. Serve at once.

From left: Avocado and pink grapefruit salad, Cucumber and strawberry salad and Date, orange and radicchio salad

Pink prawn salad with sun-dried tomatoes

Serves 4 as a starter

6 radishes, quartered

100g/4oz cooked peeled prawns

1 head of red chicory, sliced

10 sun-dried tomatoes in oil, drained and halved

half quantity Classic vinaigrette (see page 23)

8 batavia or novita lettuce leaves

❶ Mix the radishes, prawns, chicory and tomatoes, then mix in the dressing.

❷ Arrange two lettuce leaves on each of four plates, spoon over the prawn mixture and serve at once.

Spicy pineapple salad

Serves 4 as a main course

1 small ripe pineapple, peeled, cored and chopped

$\frac{1}{2}$ tsp grated fresh root ginger

$\frac{1}{2}$ tsp chilli powder

1 bunch watercress, washed and drained

1 small red pepper, seeded and sliced

3 tbsp Classic vinaigrette (see page 23)

❶ Sprinkle the pineapple evenly with the ginger and chilli powder. Toss and set aside for 10 minutes.

❷ Arrange the watercress and pepper on a plate. Top with pineapple. Pour over vinaigrette. Chill before serving.

Grilled goat's cheese with rocket and watercress

Serves 4 as a starter

2 × 65g/2$\frac{1}{2}$oz Crottins de Chavignol (hard goat's cheese)

4 slices French bread

2 handfuls each rocket and watercress

FOR THE DRESSING

3 tbsp white wine vinegar

3 tbsp olive oil

3 tbsp walnut oil

$\frac{1}{2}$ tsp wholegrain mustard

seasoning

❶ Cut the cheeses in half horizontally and place one half, cut side up, on each slice of bread. Grill for 2–3 minutes until golden brown and bubbling.

❷ Meanwhile, place the rocket and watercress in a bowl. Mix the dressing ingredients, pour over and toss lightly.

❸ Serve the cheese-topped breads at once with the dressed leaves around them.

Melon and prosciutto

Serves 4–6 as a starter

1 small melon or $\frac{1}{2}$ each of two different coloured melons

12 slices prosciutto

half quantity Classic vinaigrette, (see page 23)

1 tsp chopped fresh mint

❶ Cut the melon into thin wedges and remove the seeds and skin. Arrange the melon and prosciutto on individual plates.

❷ Mix together the vinaigrette and mint and drizzle over the melon and prosciutto. Serve at room temperature.

Avocado and pink grapefruit salad

Serves 4 as a starter

2 pink grapefruit

1 avocado

FOR THE DRESSING

6 tbsp extra virgin olive oil

4 tbsp chopped fresh parsley

seasoning

❶ Using a sharp knife, peel the skin and white pith from the grapefruit. Hold the fruit over a bowl as you work to catch the juice. Add the segments of the grapefruit to the juice in the bowl.

❷ Halve, stone and peel the avocado and thinly slice. Drop the avocado slices into the grapefruit juice so as to prevent them from turning brown.

❸ Mix together the olive oil, parsley and seasoning with 2 tablespoons of the reserved grapefruit juice.

❹ Transfer avocado and grapefruit to a serving plate with a slotted spoon, pour over the dressing and serve at once.

Cucumber and strawberry salad

Serves 4–6 as a starter

1 cucumber, peeled

225g/8oz strawberries

FOR THE DRESSING

3 tbsp raspberry vinegar

3 tbsp hazelnut oil

2 tbsp extra virgin olive oil

2 tbsp chopped fresh mint

seasoning

❶ Cut the cucumber and strawberries into thick slices, arrange in a shallow dish.

❷ Mix together the vinegar, oils, mint and seasoning. Pour over salad. Leave at room temperature for 2 hours before serving.

Indonesian salad

Serves 4–6 as a main course

225g/8oz tiny new potatoes

750g/1½lb baby carrots, scrubbed and thinly sliced

175g/6oz French beans, topped, tailed and halved

100g/4oz cauliflower florets

100g/4oz broccoli florets

100g/4oz beansprouts

FOR THE DRESSING AND GARNISH

50g/2oz shelled unsalted peanuts

5 tbsp groundnut oil

1 garlic clove, crushed

1 small fresh chilli, seeded and very finely sliced (optional)

1½ tbsp rice wine vinegar or white wine vinegar

25g/½oz creamed coconut, finely grated

seasoning

❶ Simmer the potatoes in a large pan of boiling, salted water until tender. Drain and set aside.

❷ Blanch the carrots, French beans, cauliflower and broccoli for 3–4 minutes until just tender. Drain, rinse in cold water and place in salad bowls with the potatoes and beansprouts, mixing well. Cover and chill.

❸ Fry the peanuts in 4 tablespoons of oil until golden. Add garlic and chilli and fry for a few seconds. Cool and set aside.

❹ Mix together the remaining oil and dressing ingredients. Before serving, pour this over vegetables. Sprinkle peanut mixture over the top and toss together.

Shredded Savoy salad

Serves 4–6 as a side salad

225g/8oz Savoy cabbage, finely shredded

225g/8oz Chinese leaves, finely shredded

225g/8oz carrots, very finely grated

½ a head of celery (including the leaves), finely sliced diagonally

1 small red onion or 2 small shallots, finely sliced

grated rind of 1 small orange

100g/4oz hazelnuts

FOR THE DRESSING

5 tbsp natural yogurt

5 tbsp mayonnaise

juice of 1 small orange

1 tbsp wholegrain mustard

seasoning

❶ Mix together all the ingredients for the salad and place in four or six small serving bowls. Cover and chill until ready to serve.

❷ Mix together all the ingredients for the dressing and chill until ready to serve. Pour the dressing over the salad just before serving and toss together.

Spinach salad with lentils and yogurt

Serves 6 as a main course

225g/8oz green lentils

225g/8oz red lentils

225g/8oz small spinach leaves

FOR THE DRESSING

150g/5oz natural yogurt

juice of 1 lemon

seasoning

❶ Wash the lentils separately, removing stones or discoloured lentils.

❷ Place in separate pans of cold water and bring to the boil. Simmer the red lentils for about 15 minutes and the green for about 45 minutes

until they are tender, yet still holding their shape. Drain and cool.

❸ Wash the spinach leaves and chop off any thick stalks. Place in a salad bowl. Scatter the lentils on top. Mix the yogurt, lemon juice and seasoning, pour over salad and serve.

Rocket and cauliflower salad

Serves 4 as a main course

100g/4oz rocket

1 batavia lettuce

100g/4oz cauliflower florets

FOR THE DRESSING

3 tbsp hazelnut oil

1 tsp Dijon mustard

juice of ½ lemon

50g/2oz hazelnuts, chopped and toasted

seasoning

❶ Mix the rocket and lettuce in a large bowl, and set aside.

❷ Steam the cauliflower florets for about 5 minutes until just tender, rinse in cold water, then drain and add to the salad.

❸ Put the oil, mustard, lemon juice and hazelnuts in a screw-topped jar and shake vigorously to mix. Pour over the salad just before serving and toss lightly.

Right: Smoked chicken salad

Smoked chicken salad

Serves 4–6 as a main course

1 smoked chicken, about 1.25kg/2½lb or 225g/8oz smoked turkey breast

100g/4oz smoked ham, thickly sliced

100g/4oz mangetout, sliced diagonally if large

350g/12oz tomatoes

1 peach or nectarine

300g/10oz paglia e fieno (long, thin green and white pasta)

FOR THE DRESSING

5 tbsp sunflower oil

2 tbsp olive oil

2 tbsp red wine vinegar

1 tbsp chopped fresh parsley

1 tbsp snipped fresh chives

seasoning

❶ Remove the skin from the chicken and cut the flesh into thin strips. Cut the ham and turkey, if using, into thin strips. Blanch the mangetout in boiling, salted water for 1–2 minutes. Drain and rinse in cold water.

❷ Dip the tomatoes, a few at a time, into boiling water for 30 seconds, cool in cold water, then peel off their skins. Cut tomatoes in half, remove seeds, and then cut flesh into long, thin shreds.

❸ Cut the peach or nectarine in half, remove the stones and cut the fruit into thin wedges.

❹ Cook the paglia e fieno in plenty of boiling, salted water until tender, drain and rinse in cold water.

❺ Mix together the smoked chicken or turkey, ham, mangetout and peach or nectarine and tomato and stir gently but thoroughly. Arrange in the centre of a large serving platter.

❻ Using two forks, twist the pasta into small, nest-like bundles and arrange around the sides of the salad. Cover and chill in the fridge until it's ready to be served.

❼ For the dressing, mix together the sunflower and olive oils, then add the wine vinegar. Stir in the chopped parsley and chives and season to taste. Pour the dressing over the salad just before you are ready to serve it.

Country salad

Serves 6–8 as a side salad

½ head frisée lettuce

1 small oak leaf lettuce

1 packet lamb's lettuce

2 chicory heads, cut into pieces

a selection of fresh herbs and edible flowers, such as roquette, sorrel, basil, chervil, flat leaf parsley, borage flowers, pansies, thyme flowers and nasturtiums

FOR THE DRESSING

1 tbsp sunflower oil

2 tbsp hazelnut oil

1 tbsp white wine vinegar

1 garlic clove, crushed

½ tsp French mustard

seasoning

❶ Tear the lettuces into small pieces. Put them and the other salad ingredients into large serving bowl and toss together. Cover and chill until ready to serve.

❷ Mix dressing ingredients. Pour over the salad before serving and toss well.

Tomato and seed salad

Serves 4 as a side salad

450g/1lb tomatoes, cut into wedges

1 tbsp chopped fresh chives

2 tbsp sunflower seeds, toasted

2 tbsp pumpkin seeds, toasted

FOR THE DRESSING

3 tbsp olive oil

2 tbsp sunflower or grapeseed oil

2 tbsp white wine or raspberry vinegar

$\frac{1}{2}$ tsp coarse-grain mustard

seasoning

❶ Place the tomatoes in a dish with the chives and seeds. Shake the dressing ingredients together in a screw-topped jar and pour over the tomatoes. Toss gently to mix and serve within an hour.

Oyster mushroom and tomato salad

Serves 6 as a side salad

225g/8oz oyster mushrooms

450g/1lb tomatoes, sliced

2 tbsp chopped fresh parsley

FOR THE DRESSING

10 tbsp sunflower oil

8 tbsp white wine vinegar

seasoning

1 red pepper

squeeze of lemon juice

pinch of ground cumin

2 tbsp olive oil

❶ Put the mushrooms, tomatoes and parsley in a medium salad bowl. Mix together the sunflower oil, 4 tablespoons of the vinegar, add the seasoning, and pour over the salad. Toss and leave to marinate for 1 hour, gently tossing from time to time.

❷ Meanwhile, halve and seed the pepper and char under the grill. Place the pepper in a polythene bag for about 10 minutes. Peel off the blackened skin and cut the pepper into chunks.

❸ Whizz the pepper in a blender with the remaining dressing ingredients. Spoon over the salad and serve at once.

Below: Tomato and seed salad

Smoked fish salad with herb dressing

Serves 4 as a main course

FOR THE DRESSING

6 tbsp olive oil

grated rind and juice of $\frac{1}{2}$ lemon

$\frac{1}{2}$ tsp golden caster sugar

4 tbsp chopped fresh herbs, such as chives, parsley, dill, tarragon and chervil

seasoning

FOR THE SALAD

2 smoked trout fillets

1 peppered mackerel fillet

100g/4oz smoked salmon

small piece of smoked cod's roe, thinly sliced

pickled dill cucumbers, thinly sliced

sprigs of fresh herbs, to garnish

❶ First, mix together all of the dressing ingredients; set aside.

❷ Flake the trout and mackerel fillets into small pieces. Cut the smoked salmon into strips. Arrange the fish and cod's roe on plates with the dill cucumbers. Spoon the dressing on top and serve the salad garnished with sprigs of fresh herbs.

Minted skate salad

Serves 3–4 as a main course

450g/1lb skate wings

4 tbsp sweet white wine

$\frac{1}{4}$ cucumber, cut into small matchsticks

1 red pepper, seeded and cut into small matchsticks

2 tbsp white wine vinegar

1 tsp golden caster sugar

1 tbsp chopped fresh mint

seasoning

mixed salad leaves and warm bread, to serve

❶ Place the skate wings and wine in a pan. Cover and simmer for 8 minutes on each side until the thickest part is cooked through. Drain and shred the flesh of the fish from the cartilage.

❷ Gently cook the cucumber and pepper in the vinegar and sugar for about 3 minutes until softened.

❸ Transfer the cucumber and pepper to a large bowl and stir in the skate, mint and seasoning. Pack the mixture into individual mousse tins or ramekin dishes and chill for several hours or overnight.

❹ Turn out each ramekin on to a serving plate, surround with a few mixed salad leaves and serve with warm bread.

Spiced seafood salad

Serves 4 as a main course

FOR THE SALAD

1kg/2lb fresh mussels, scrubbed

450g/1lb whole prawns

1 bag mixed salad leaves

2 tbsp olive oil

seasoning

FOR THE DRESSING

$\frac{1}{2}$ tsp coriander seeds

$\frac{1}{2}$ tsp cumin seeds

$\frac{1}{4}$ tsp fennel seeds

$\frac{1}{4}$ tsp ground turmeric

1 tsp wholegrain mustard

good pinch of chilli powder

4 tbsp single cream

pickled sweet chillies, to garnish

❶ To make the salad, discard any damaged mussels and those that remain open when tapped. Steam them in 4 tablespoons of water until they have opened. Drain, discarding any that remain closed. Remove most of them from their shells, then leave to cool.

❷ Put 8 prawns aside and carefully peel the rest, leaving the tails on. Toss all the mussels with the peeled prawns and salad leaves in the oil and season lightly. Divide among four large plates.

❸ To make the dressing, lightly crush the coriander, cumin and fennel seeds. Mix with remaining dressing ingredients, season well and spoon over the salad. Serve garnished with the reserved whole prawns and pickled sweet chillies.

Spiced tuna salad Niçoise

Serves 4 as a main course

175g/6oz French beans

175g/6oz frozen broad beans

2 tbsp olive oil

1 large onion, sliced

2 garlic cloves, crushed

1–2 tsp curry paste

200g/7oz can tuna in brine, drained and flaked

350g/12oz tomatoes, cut into wedges

12 black olives

seasoning

❶ Trim the French beans and cut them into 4cm/1$\frac{1}{2}$in lengths. Bring a pan of salted water to the boil and cook the French beans and broad beans for 2 minutes. Drain and set aside.

❷ Heat the oil in a large pan and gently fry the onion and garlic for 5 minutes. Stir in the curry paste and cook for 1 minute.

❸ Add the beans to the pan with the tuna flakes, tomatoes and black olives, then season to taste. Gently heat through, lightly tossing the ingredients together, and serve immediately.

Eggs

*Cracking good recipes for eggs that just
can't be beaten! Savoury and sweet omelettes,
soufflés, meringues and roulades with
easy-to-follow instructions – exactly what
you need for foolproof results.*

Leek omelette

Serves 4–6

675g/1½lb leeks
50g/2oz butter
juice of 1 lemon
seasoning
6 eggs
25g/1oz Gruyère, grated

① Wash and trim the leeks. Be sure to get rid of the soil by making slashes where you see grit under the layers and rinsing under running water. Slice into thin rings.

② Melt the butter in a heavy-based frying pan (which has a handle that won't melt under a grill) and fry the leeks until soft. Add the lemon juice and season well.

③ Meanwhile, beat the eggs in a large bowl. Add the leeks and Gruyère. Pour the mixture back into the pan and cook over a gentle heat for about 15 minutes until set.

④ Transfer the pan to the grill and cook for about 5 minutes or until the omelette has turned a golden brown and has completely set underneath.

⑤ Leave the omelette in the pan for 5 minutes. Loosen with a palette knife, then carefully slide out on to a serving dish. Serve hot or cold in wedges.

From left: Leek omelette, Spicy chicken omelette and Cherry and almond omelette (recipes overleaf)

Spicy chicken omelette

This omelette is good served hot or cold in wedges, and is great for picnics and *hors d'oeuvres*.

Serves 4–6
25g/1oz butter
1 medium onion, finely chopped
1 garlic clove, crushed
450g/1lb cooked chicken, diced
1 tsp each ground cumin and coriander
1 tbsp chopped fresh coriander
1 tbsp pine nuts
6 eggs
seasoning
a little Greek strained yogurt, to serve

❶ Melt the butter in a heavy-based frying pan (which has a handle that won't melt when placed under a grill) and fry the onion and garlic until softened. Add the diced chicken and fry until browned, stirring frequently.
❷ Leave the chicken mixture to cool slightly in the pan. Stir in the ground spices, coriander and pine nuts. Season well.
❸ Beat the eggs and pour into the pan and cook over a gentle heat for about 15 minutes until set.
❹ Preheat the grill to a medium heat and place the frying pan underneath. Cook for about 5 minutes or until the top is set and golden brown. Serve the omelette hot or cold in wedges accompanied by Greek strained yogurt.

Cherry and almond omelette

It may sound unusual, but why not try a sweet omelette for a change? It is quick to make and tastes rather like a fruit and custard-type dessert. You could try this recipe with sliced apples or pears, or tinned apricots that have been well drained.

Serves 4–6
50g/2oz butter
675g/1½lb cherries, stoned, or 2 × 425g/15oz cans pitted black cherries, drained
4 eggs
100g/4oz natural low-fat fromage frais
25g/1oz caster sugar
25g/1oz ground almonds
few drops almond essence
25g/1oz flaked almonds
icing sugar, to decorate

❶ Melt the butter, in a heavy-based frying pan (which has a handle that won't melt when placed under a grill). Add the cherries to the frying pan and cook for 3–4 minutes until they are slightly soft.
❷ Beat the eggs into the fromage frais. Add sugar, ground almonds and almond essence and mix well. Pour over the cherries in the pan. Stir and cook gently for 8–10 minutes until set.
❸ Preheat the grill to a medium heat. Sprinkle the flaked almonds over the top of the omelette, place the pan under the grill and cook until the top of the omelette is set and golden brown. Serve warm, dusted with icing sugar.

Cheese soufflé

Always whisk egg whites stiffly, ensure base is the right consistency and fold together well.

Serves 4
65g/2½oz butter
50g/2oz plain flour
300ml/½ pint milk
75g/3oz mature Cheddar, grated
4 eggs, separated
1 tsp Dijon mustard
seasoning

❶ Preheat the oven to 200C/400F/Gas 6. Melt 10g/¼oz of the butter and brush over the inside of a large, ovenproof soufflé dish, ensuring that the dish is buttered very evenly.
❷ Melt the remaining butter in a large pan, stir in the flour and cook for 1 minute. Add the milk and cook over a medium heat, stirring continuously until the mixture is thickened and smooth.
❸ Remove the pan from the heat, add the cheese and stir until melted. Beat together the egg yolks, then beat them into the sauce along with the mustard and plenty of seasoning. Set aside.
❹ Whisk the egg whites until stiff but not dry, then mix a spoonful into the cheese sauce. Carefully fold in the remaining egg whites using a metal spoon and pour into the prepared soufflé dish.
❺ Bake for 25–30 minutes until well risen and golden brown. Check the soufflé by opening the oven door very slightly and nudging the dish – if the soufflé is very wobbly, cook for a few more minutes.

Twice-baked cheese soufflés

Serves 4

65g/2½oz butter

40g/1½oz plain flour

300ml/½ pint milk

25g/1oz Gruyère, grated

2 tbsp grated Parmesan

3 eggs, separated

¼ tsp paprika

200ml/7fl oz double cream

seasoning

1 Preheat the oven to 180C/350F/ Gas 4. Melt the butter and use 1 tablespoon to grease four ramekins. Stir flour into the remaining butter and cook for 1 minute. Gradually pour in the milk and cook, stirring continuously until thickened.

2 Remove pan from heat, add half each of the Gruyère and Parmesan. Stir to melt, beat in yolks, paprika and seasoning.

3 Whisk the egg whites until stiff but not dry and mix a spoonful into the cheese sauce. Fold in the remaining egg whites with a metal spoon and carefully pour into the prepared ramekins.

4 Place all four ramekins in a deep roasting tin, then pour in boiling water to come half way up the sides. Bake for 15–20 minutes or until golden brown. Carefully turn them out into four greased, individual gratin dishes.

5 Pour cream over soufflés, sprinkle over remaining cheese. Bake 10–15 minutes until puffed and golden. Serve at once.

Hot chocolate soufflés

Butter the dish evenly, especially around the rim, so the soufflé can slip easily up the edges. Slide round the tip of a knife in between the mixture and the dish before cooking.

Serves 4

90g/3½oz butter, softened

65g/2½oz, plus 4 tsp caster sugar

300ml/½ pint milk

4 eggs, separated

25g/1oz cornflour

50g/2oz plain flour

1 tbsp instant coffee granules

75g/3oz dark chocolate, grated

icing sugar, to decorate

1 Preheat the oven to 180C/350F/ Gas 4. Melt 15g/½oz of the butter and use to grease four 300ml/½ pint soufflé dishes. Sprinkle the insides of the dishes evenly with 1 tablespoon of the sugar.

2 Heat the milk until almost boiling, then remove from the heat. Whisk the yolks with the remaining sugar (not the 4 teaspoons) until pale and light. Whisk in both types of flour, then gradually stir in the milk. Return to pan, heat and stir continuously until thickened.

3 Dissolve the coffee granules in 1 tablespoon of boiling water and stir into the mixture. Add the chocolate and remaining butter and stir until melted. Leave the mixture to cool slightly.

4 Whisk the egg whites until they form soft peaks. Beat in the 4 teaspoons of caster sugar until stiff but not dry. Mix a spoonful of this egg white mixture into the chocolate custard, then carefully fold in the remainder.

5 Pour the mixture into the prepared soufflé dishes. Bake for about 20 minutes until well risen and just soft in the centre. Dust the soufflés with a little icing sugar and serve immediately.

Right: Hot chocolate soufflés

BASIC SPINACH ROULADE

Fill cold roulades with mayonnaise, hot ones with white sauce and smoked fish, prawns or chopped boiled egg.

Serves 4

150g/5oz frozen, chopped spinach

15g/½oz butter

4 eggs, separated

a little freshly grated nutmeg

seasoning

2 tbsp grated Parmesan

❶ Preheat the oven to 190C/375F/Gas 5. Gently cook the spinach in a covered pan for 8 minutes. Remove the lid to evaporate any excess liquid, then beat in the butter.

❷ Line a 20 × 30cm/8 × 12in roulade tin with non-stick baking paper and clip folded sides to form a wall. Beat the egg yolks into the spinach, then season with nutmeg, salt and pepper.

Carrot roulade

Serves 6

100g/4oz butter

675g/1½lb carrots, finely grated

6 eggs, separated

seasoning

FOR THE FILLING

6 hard-boiled eggs, finely chopped

300ml/½ pint mayonnaise

2 tbsp chopped fresh dill

❶ Preheat the oven to 200C/400F/Gas 6. Line a 20 × 30cm/8 × 12in roulade tin with non-stick baking paper. Set aside.
❷ Melt the butter in a pan, add the carrots and cook gently until soft. Remove the pan from the heat, beat in the egg yolks and season well.
❸ Whisk the egg whites until stiff but not dry. Carefully fold into the carrot mixture with a metal spoon. Pour the mixture into the prepared tin and spread until smooth. Bake for 10 minutes until golden brown and springy to the touch. Cover with a damp cloth and leave to cool before filling.

❹ Mix the hard-boiled eggs with the mayonnaise and dill and season well. Turn out the roulade on to a sheet of non-stick baking paper. Carefully peel off the lining paper and spread the filling over the roulade, leaving a 1cm/½in border all around the edge.
❺ Starting at one shorter side, roll up the roulade very carefully, using the paper to help you. Trim the ends to neaten it and serve the roulade cut into slices.

From left: Carrot roulade, Basic spinach roulade and Hazelnut roulade

❸ Whisk egg whites until stiff but not dry and fold into spinach mixture. Spread evenly in the tin and sprinkle the top with 1 tablespoon of the Parmesan.

❹ Bake for 10–12 minutes until firm, then remove from the oven and cover with a damp cloth. Turn out on to greaseproof paper sprinkled with remaining Parmesan.

❺ Remove lining paper and cover the roulade with your chosen filling, leaving a 1cm/$\frac{1}{2}$in border. Starting at shorter side, roll up using the paper, and trim ends.

Hazelnut roulade

Serves 4–6

4 eggs, separated

65g/2$\frac{1}{2}$oz caster sugar

65g/2$\frac{1}{2}$oz ground hazelnuts

150ml/$\frac{1}{4}$ pint double cream

100g/4oz fresh or frozen raspberries

icing sugar, to decorate

❶ Preheat the oven to 180C/350F/Gas 4. Line a 20 × 30cm/8 × 12in roulade tin with non-stick baking paper.

❷ Place the egg yolks and sugar in a bowl over a pan of gently simmering water and whisk until it is pale and thick. Remove from heat and whisk until it cools and has almost trebled in volume.

❸ Whisk the egg whites until stiff but not dry. Fold into the yolks along with the ground hazelnuts.

❹ Spread into the prepared tin and bake for 10–12 minutes until firm and golden. Turn out on to greaseproof paper sprinkled with

icing sugar. Peel off the lining paper and trim the edges. Cover and leave to cool.

❺ Whip the cream so it forms soft peaks and spread evenly over the roulade, leaving a 1cm/$\frac{1}{2}$in border all around the edge. Dot with raspberries. Roll up from one shorter side, using the paper to help you. Dredge with a little icing sugar.

Floating islands

Serves 4

FOR THE CUSTARD

5 egg yolks

450ml/$\frac{3}{4}$ pint milk

50g/2oz caster sugar

few drops vanilla essence

FOR THE MERINGUE

2 egg whites

50g/2oz caster sugar

FOR THE CARAMEL

4 tbsp caster sugar

❶ Mix the egg yolks, milk and sugar in a bowl. Set bowl over a pan of simmering water and heat gently for about 15 minutes, stirring constantly, until mixture coats the back of a wooden spoon.

❷ Stir in the vanilla essence and place mixture in four individual glasses or one large dish. Cover; chill for 2 hours.

❸ Whisk egg whites in a clean, grease-free bowl until they stand in stiff peaks. Gradually whisk in two-thirds of the sugar, then fold in the remainder.

❹ Spoon eight large spoonfuls of meringue into a pan of simmering water. Poach gently for about 5 minutes until set. Remove with a slotted spoon, drain on kitchen paper and spoon on to custard.

❺ Melt the sugar for the caramel in a small, heavy-based pan until it turns golden. Remove from heat, cool slightly and drizzle over meringues.

Grape meringue tart

Serves 4–6

3 egg whites

175g/6oz caster sugar, plus 1 tbsp for dusting

350g/12oz grapes, seeded

75g/3oz ground almonds

20cm/8in precooked shortcrust pastry case

❶ Preheat the oven to 180C/350F/Gas 4. Whisk the egg whites until stiff. Gradually whisk in 100g/4oz of the sugar, then fold in the remainder.

❷ Fold in grapes and ground almonds alternately, then spoon into the pastry case. Sprinkle with the final tablespoon of sugar. Bake for 50 minutes until pale golden.

Walnut meringues

Serves 6

4 egg whites

225g/8oz light muscovado sugar

few drops vanilla essence

½ tsp vinegar

75g/3oz walnuts, very finely chopped

ice cream or whipped cream, to serve

❶ Preheat the oven to 190C/ 375F/Gas 5. Line a large baking sheet with some non-stick baking paper.

❷ Whisk the egg whites until stiff. Gradually beat in the sugar, vanilla and vinegar. Beat until very stiff and shiny, then fold in the walnuts.

❸ Spoon mounds of meringue on to the baking sheet and bake for about 30 minutes until light brown. Serve with ice cream or sandwich with whipped cream.

Pineapple Pavlova

Serves 8

225g/8oz caster sugar

4 egg whites

1 tsp cornflour

½ tsp vinegar

few drops vanilla essence

1 medium pineapple, peeled, cored and cut into chunks

300ml/½ pint double cream, whipped

seeds and pulp of 2 passion fruit

❶ Preheat the oven to 140C/275F/Gas 1. Line a baking sheet with non-stick baking paper, and dust with caster sugar.

❷ Whisk egg whites until stiff, add half of the sugar and whisk again until smooth and shiny. Whisk in the remaining sugar, cornflour, vinegar and vanilla essence.

❸ Using a palette knife, spread meringue into a round on the baking sheet. Bake for about 50 minutes until pale brown. Cool.

❹ Remove lining paper and slide Pavlova on to a serving dish. Fold half the pineapple into the cream and spread on meringue. Top with passion fruit and pineapple.

From left: Floating islands, Grape meringue tart and Walnut meringues

Pasta

Economical and versatile, pasta comes in all shapes and sizes. Make your own or use a dried shop-bought variety. Serve with the delicious sauces or stuffings found here, or invent your own.

Tagliatelle Bolognese

Serves 4

2-egg quantity Egg pasta (see page 45)

75g/3oz Gruyère, grated

2 tbsp grated Parmesan

FOR THE SAUCE

2 tbsp olive oil

1 small onion, finely chopped

1 carrot, finely chopped

1 celery stick, finely chopped

100g/4oz pancetta or unsmoked bacon, cut crossways into thin shreds

1 garlic clove, crushed

350g/12oz minced beef

150ml/$\frac{1}{4}$ pint dry white wine

225g/8oz can chopped tomatoes

2 tbsp tomato purée

seasoning

❶ To make the sauce, heat the oil in a large pan, add the onion, carrot and celery and cook over a medium heat until soft. Add the pancetta or bacon, garlic and beef and cook until browned.

❷ Add the wine and cook to reduce by half. Add the tomatoes, purée and seasoning. Bring to the boil, cover and simmer for 45–60 minutes. Add water if it is too thick.

❸ To make the tagliatelle, roll out the dough thinly by hand or machine to the narrowest but one setting. Lay sheets on tea towels, with one third of their length hung over the work surface edge. Leave for 30 minutes until dry to the touch yet still pliable.

❹ Feed sheets through 5mm/$\frac{1}{4}$in cutters, or thinly slice to make strands. Separate; spread on floured tea towels.

❺ Pour sauce into a shallow, ovenproof dish and keep warm. Cook pasta until just firm to bite. Drain, place on top of sauce. Cover with cheeses and grill until golden.

From left: Fettuccine with Italian sausage and peppers (recipe page 46) and Tagliatelle Bolognese

Shaping up

Dried, shop-bought pasta is completely different from fresh pasta as it is made from durum wheat flour and water. Spaghetti is still the most popular shape even though there are now more than 100 others. Dried pasta is an excellent stand-by to have in your cupboard; if you keep it dry, it will last almost indefinitely. Cook in the same way as fresh pasta but check the packet for cooking times, test it and drain when it is just firm to the bite. Serve at once with the sauce – don't ever leave pasta to wait before it is eaten.

The main pasta shapes to look for are pictured above, clockwise from top right: farfalle, white and green spaghetti, ruote, penne, green and white tagliatelle, rigatoni, lumache, conchiglie (for stuffing), short cut macaroni, conchiglie, chiocciole (in centre), fusilli in three colours, vermicelli, ondule. Names may vary among manufacturers.

Simple sauces

A pasta sauce can be as simple as a drizzle of olive oil and a scattering of Parmesan, but cream sauces are extra tasty. Pasta sauces suit particular shapes – long thin strands are kept separate with light olive oil or egg-based sauces. Thick strips, such as tagliatelle, support cheese and meat sauces, while tubes go well with vegetable sauces. Lasagne and short pasta, such as macaroni, are best for rich, baked dishes.

Béchamel sauce
Melt 25g/1oz butter in a pan, add 25g/1oz plain flour, cook for 1 minute. Gradually add 600ml/

1 pint milk and cook, stirring until boiling and thick. Season; simmer gently for 10 minutes.

Tomato and basil sauce
Chop 25g/1oz fresh basil leaves and cook with 400g/14oz can of chopped tomatoes, 1 tablespoon tomato purée, 2 crushed garlic cloves, 2 tablespoons olive oil and seasoning for 15 minutes.

Prosciutto and cream sauce
Soften 1 chopped shallot in 25g/1oz unsalted butter and 2 tablespoons olive oil. Add 75g/3oz shredded prosciutto, cook for 2 minutes. Add 6 tablespoons dry white wine, bring to boil and reduce heat. Add 300ml/½ pint single cream and 3 tablespoons grated Parmesan. Simmer and season with black pepper.

Herb and garlic sauce
Heat 4 tablespoons olive oil in a pan, add 2 crushed garlic cloves and 1–2 tablespoons each of chopped fresh parsley, basil, marjoram, thyme and fennel. Cook for 1–2 minutes.

Pink prawn sauce
Fry 2 crushed garlic cloves in 4 tablespoons olive oil, add 1 tablespoon sun-dried tomato purée and 6 tablespoons dry white wine. Simmer for 2–3 minutes, add 100g/4oz cooked, shelled prawns and cook for 2 minutes. Purée in a food processor, then return to the pan and add 300ml/½ pint single cream. Season to taste and reheat gently.

Gorgonzola sauce
Melt 25g/1oz butter in a pan, stir in 1 crushed garlic clove, cook for 1 minute. Add 200g/7oz Gorgonzola in small bits and 150ml/¼ pint single cream. Cook, stirring, until cheese is melting. Grind over black pepper, grate over nutmeg.

HOME-MADE PASTA

If stored, fresh pasta should be left to dry out completely after being made and placed in an airtight bag or box. Always wind long strands, such as tagliatelle, into nests while they are still pliable.

Egg pasta

Serves 2
175g/6oz unbleached plain flour
2 eggs

❶ Heap 150g/5oz of the flour on to a work surface, spread it slightly and make a well in the middle. Break eggs into well, work in the flour to form a dough with fingers. Add more flour if it's too wet.

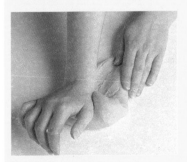

❷ Scrape the work surface clean, sprinkle with flour and knead dough for 5–8 minutes until it becomes smooth and elastic. Divide the dough into four equal pieces.

❸ Roll dough five or six times through the widest setting on a pasta machine, fold and half turn it each time. Or rest dough, covered, for 15–30 minutes and use a rolling pin to roll, fold and turn several times.

❹ When the dough is smooth, run it unfolded through the rollers, closing them one notch at a time, or roll out by hand until you get the required thickness, then follow individual pasta recipes.

Careful cooking
Leave fresh pasta to dry before cooking to prevent sticking. Bring 1.2 litres/2 pints of water to the boil with 1 teaspoon of salt for each 100g/4oz of pasta. Add pasta, stir and cook until slightly firm to the bite. Strands of fresh pasta will be ready when the water returns to the boil; stuffed pasta takes a few minutes. Once cooked, pour a cupful of cold water into the pan (before draining) to stop further cooking. Reserve a cupful of cooking liquid to add to the sauce as it is very absorbent.

FLAVOURED PASTA

Originally, pasta was always yellow and unflavoured, except for the long-standing use of spinach to make *pasta verde* (green pasta). Although many traditional Italian cooks dismiss flavourings as a passing fad now, fresh pasta does lend itself to additions such as tomato purée, chopped herbs, crushed garlic or a dash of white wine or olive oil.

❶ For **spinach pasta,** thaw 150g/5oz frozen chopped spinach, squeeze dry, add to 2 eggs and 225g/8oz plain flour. For **tomato pasta,** mix 3 tbsp tomato purée, 2 eggs and 200g/7oz plain flour.

❷ Lasagne and cannelloni are flat sheets and are easy to roll by hand after the initial rolling and folding. If you use a machine, run through the prepared dough unfolded, right down to the thinnest setting.

❸ For **lasagne,** cut the pasta sheets to 12 × 9cm/5 × 3½in. For **cannelloni,** cut to 10 × 7.5cm/4 × 3in. Can be cooked in batches or dried on floured tea towels.

❹ For **garganelli,** roll out the pasta a piece at a time to the thinnest setting, then cut into 4cm/1½in squares. Place one square diagonally on a ridged butter bat or on a large, clean comb.

❺ Roll up the square using a length of dowelling, pressing down gently to form a ridged tube. Slide the tube off the dowelling and leave to dry on a tea towel. Repeat until all the dough is used up.

Fettuccine with Italian sausage and peppers

Serves 2

1-egg quantity Egg pasta (see page 45)

1-egg quantity spinach-flavoured pasta (see step 1 left)

FOR THE SAUCE

2 tbsp olive oil

1 small onion, finely chopped

1 red and 1 yellow pepper, seeded and cut into 2.5cm/1in squares

425g/15oz can chopped tomatoes

2 tbsp tomato purée

225g/8oz Italian sausage, sliced

seasoning

❶ To make the fettucine roll out each dough thinly by hand or machine to the narrowest but one setting. Lay sheets on tea towels, with one third of their length hung over the work surface edge. Leave for 30 minutes until dry to the touch yet still pliable.

❷ Meanwhile heat oil and fry the onion and peppers until soft, add the tomatoes, purée and seasoning. Simmer for 15 minutes.

❸ Cook the sausage in 4 tablespoons of water until water has evaporated and sausages are browned. Add to sauce and simmer.

❹ Cut pasta into strips 2cm/¾in wide separate and spread on floured tea towels. Cook the white and green pasta separately until tender. Drain, mix and cover with sauce.

Spinach-stuffed lasagne rolls

Serves 4
2-egg quantity Egg pasta (see page 45), made into lasagne sheets
1-egg quantity tomato-flavoured pasta (see page 46, step 1) made into lasagne sheets
300ml/$\frac{1}{2}$ pint Béchamel sauce (see page 44)
50g/2oz Gruyère, grated
FOR THE FILLING
225g/8oz sliced ham, finely chopped
350g/12oz frozen chopped spinach, thawed and squeezed dry
225g/8oz ricotta
6 tbsp grated Parmesan
1 egg, plus 1 egg yolk
pinch of grated nutmeg
seasoning

❶ Halve each lasagne sheet lengthways. Roll a wooden skewer in a backwards and forwards motion over one long edge of each sheet to flute it. Cook in batches in a large pan of boiling, salted water until almost tender and then remove carefully with a slotted spoon.
❷ Preheat the oven to 180C/350F/Gas 4. Mix together the filling ingredients, spread a little down the centre of each pasta strip and roll up loosely. Arrange the rolls, with fluted edges pointing upwards, in a 20 × 25cm/8 × 10in ovenproof dish. Pour over Béchamel sauce, sprinkle with Gruyère and bake for 20 minutes until golden.

Garganelli with aubergine

Serves 4
1 aubergine, diced
4 tbsp olive oil
$\frac{1}{2}$ small onion, chopped
1 garlic clove, crushed
2-egg quantity spinach-flavoured pasta, made into garganelli (page 46, steps 1 and 4)
4 tbsp chopped fresh parsley
$\frac{1}{4}$ tsp ground cinnamon
seasoning

❶ Place the aubergine in a colander, sprinkle with salt and leave to drain for 30 minutes. Rinse very thoroughly and then squeeze dry with your hands. Heat the oil in a large frying pan, add the aubergine, onion and garlic and fry until soft.
❷ Meanwhile, cook the garganelli in plenty of boiling, salted water until almost done. Drain well and toss into the frying pan with the parsley, cinnamon and seasoning. Stir together over the heat for about a minute, then serve immediately.

From left: Spinach-stuffed lasagne rolls and Garganelli with aubergine

Cappelletti with pink prawn sauce

Serves 4

2-egg quantity Egg pasta (see page 45)

Pink prawn sauce (see page 45)

2 tbsp shredded fresh basil, to garnish

FOR THE FILLING

2 shallots, 1 celery stick, 1 small carrot, all chopped

225g/8oz cod fillet

3 tbsp white wine

1 egg yolk

2 tbsp grated Parmesan

1 tbsp chopped fresh parsley

a little grated nutmeg

seasoning

❶ To make the filling, place the shallots, celery and carrot in a shallow pan, lay fish on top and pour over the wine and 150ml/$\frac{1}{4}$ pint water. Simmer for 12–15 minutes.

❷ Cool and remove fish skin and bones. Blend fish, yolk, cheese and parsley in a food processor for 30 seconds. Add nutmeg and season.

❸ Cut and fill cappelletti (see Stuffed pasta page 49, steps 1–2), and cook in boiling, salted water until just firm to bite. Serve with Pink prawn sauce and basil garnish.

Spinach ravioli with prosciutto and cream sauce

Serves 4

spinach-flavoured pasta made with 3 eggs, 350g/12oz plain flour and 200g/7oz spinach (see page 46, step 1)

Prosciutto and cream sauce (see page 45)

FOR THE FILLING

15g/$\frac{1}{2}$ oz dried porcini mushrooms (optional)

100g/4oz button mushrooms

2 tbsp olive oil

175g/6oz minced pork

1 egg yolk

75g/3oz ricotta

2 tbsp grated Parmesan

seasoning

❶ Soak the dried mushrooms in warm water for 30 minutes. Slice the button mushrooms. Heat the oil and brown the pork. Drain mushrooms and add to the pork with the button mushrooms. Fry for 10–15 minutes, then leave to cool.
❷ Blend the pork mixture in a food processor with the remaining ingredients.
❸ Make the ravioli (see Stuffed pasta step 4 below). Cook until the pasta is *al dente*. Drain, cover with the sauce and serve at once.

From left: Cappelletti with pink prawn sauce and Spinach ravioli with prosciutto and cream sauce

STUFFED PASTA

Stuffed pasta is very easy to make – but takes a while to prepare.

Add 1 teaspoon of olive oil when making a quantity of Egg pasta dough (see page 45) to help soften and stick edges together. Spinach and tomato pasta do not need oil added as they are already soft enough.

When making stuffed pasta (or *pasta ripieni*), only cut a few shapes at a time and keep the remaining pasta pliable by covering it with a tea towel.

❶ To make **cappelletti,** cut a 4cm/1½in wide strip of pasta, then cut into 4cm/1½in squares. Keep the rest of the pasta under a dry tea towel. Place ¼ teaspoon of filling in the centre of each square.

❷ Fold each square almost in half on the diagonal. Press sides to seal. Hold one corner on the long side between thumb and index finger. Wrap around and press two corners together. Leave to dry.

❸ **Tortellini** are made in the same way as cappelletti except that the pasta is cut into rounds, using a 5cm/2in cutter. When folding the pasta over, make sure the edges don't come exactly together.

❹ For **ravioli,** roll dough into two thin sheets. Brush one with beaten egg white and place spoonfuls of filling in lines on top. Cover with second sheet, seal around filling. Cut squares with a pastry wheel.

❺ You can make stuffed pasta shapes up to a day before they are cooked. Spread out on a dry tea towel in a cool place, make sure that none are touching and turn them occasionally until dry.

Conchiglie with peas and crispy bacon

Serves 4

350g/12oz conchiglie (shells)
225g/8oz smoked streaky bacon
100g/4oz soft cheese with garlic and herbs
150ml/$\frac{1}{4}$ pint single cream
100g/4oz frozen peas
fresh Parmesan shavings, to serve
seasoning

❶ Cook the pasta in plenty of boiling, salted water for about 10 minutes until just firm to bite.
❷ Meanwhile, make the sauce. Grill the bacon until crisp, then drain on kitchen paper and chop or crumble. Melt the soft cheese with the cream over a low heat, stirring all the time until it forms a smooth sauce. Stir in the peas and cook gently for about 3 minutes until they are cooked.
❸ Stir in half the bacon and toss with the drained pasta. Serve on warm plates, sprinkled with the remaining bacon, Parmesan and black pepper.

Spaghetti with tuna and anchovies

Serves 4

350g/12oz spaghetti
4 tbsp olive oil
1 onion, chopped
1 tsp capers, chopped
6 anchovy fillets, chopped
pinch of chilli powder
100g/4oz cherry tomatoes, halved
2 tsp tomato purée
2 tbsp chopped fresh parsley
seasoning
200g/7oz can tuna in oil

❶ Cook the spaghetti in plenty of boiling, salted water for about 10 minutes until just firm to bite.
❷ Meanwhile, heat the oil in a pan, add the onion and fry for about 5 minutes until softened. Stir in capers and anchovies, then add the chilli, tomatoes, purée, parsley and seasoning and cook for 3 minutes.
❸ Flake the tuna, stir into the sauce with the oil from the can and heat through. Toss with the drained pasta and serve.

Penne with prawns and sweetcorn

For a special treat, try large tiger prawns – although they are costly, they look most attractive.

Serves 4

350g/12oz penne (tubes)
1 tbsp olive oil
25g/1 oz butter
1 garlic clove, crushed
1 red pepper, seeded and chopped
175g/6oz peeled prawns, thawed if frozen
1 tbsp pine nuts
175g/6 oz canned or frozen sweetcorn
$\frac{1}{2}$ tsp paprika
1 tsp lemon juice
1 tbsp chopped fresh parsley
seasoning

❶ Cook the penne in plenty of boiling, salted water for about 10 minutes until just firm to bite.
❷ Meanwhile, heat the oil and butter, add the garlic and red pepper and fry until softened. Stir in the prawns and pine nuts and heat through. Add the corn and cook for 5 minutes.
❸ Stir in the paprika, lemon juice, parsley and seasoning. Toss into drained pasta and serve.

Mediterranean vegetable pasta

Try making this tasty dish with fresh garlic and herb-flavoured tagliatelle – but bear in mind that the cooking time will be much shorter.

Serves 4

1 aubergine
seasoning
1 onion
3 courgettes
1 red pepper
1 yellow pepper
2 garlic cloves, chopped
4 tbsp olive oil
350g/12oz green and white tagliatelle
100g/4oz feta cheese, crumbled
freshly grated Parmesan, to serve

❶ Slice the aubergine, place in a colander and sprinkle with salt. Leave to drain for 30 minutes, rinse and dry with kitchen paper.
❷ Meanwhile, preheat the oven to 200C/400F/Gas 6.Slice the onion into eight wedges through the root. Trim the courgettes, cut in half, then slice lengthways. Halve and seed peppers, then cut each half into four thick strips.
❸ Place all the vegetables in a roasting tin and toss with the garlic, oil and seasoning. Bake for 40 minutes until they are just starting to brown.
❹ Meanwhile, bring a pan of salted water to the boil and cook the pasta for about 10 minutes until just firm to bite. Drain well, then add the pasta and feta cheese to the roasting tin and toss with the vegetables. Serve sprinkled with Parmesan and black pepper.

From top: Conchiglie with peas and crispy bacon and Penne with prawns and sweetcorn

Fish

Now that there is such a wide range of fish available, and it's so easy to cook, why not try some of the more exotic and exciting dishes we have featured here?

Fish facts

When buying fish, make sure it is absolutely fresh. Eyes should be bright, not sunken and dull, and flesh must be moist and firm. Fresh fish has a clean sea air smell; unpleasant-smelling fish should be avoided. Stale fish will quickly fall apart during cooking and will lack flavour. Vividly coloured fish should still display their colour – check for bright spots on plaice. For maximum flavour and goodness, eat fish on the day of purchase. Clean and fillet just before cooking and don't forget to use the bones and heads to make a good, wholesome stock (it freezes well). Loosely cover prepared fish and always store in refrigerator. Your fishmonger will clean and gut the fish for you, but make sure you tell him or her that you want the head or the scales left on. The head is best left on if you are cooking the whole fish as it holds the body together. The scales offer protection to the delicate flesh if you are barbecuing fish. The skin, along with the scales, can be peeled off after barbecuing. With regard to other cooking methods the scales are best removed first.

To scale a fish, first cut off the fins with a sharp pair of scissors, but take care as many of the more exotic fish have quite sharp spikes. Scales are easily removed by rubbing the blunt edge of a knife down the length of the fish – do this working from tail to head. It can be quite messy, so cover your hands and shield the fish with a sheet of newspaper or polythene to catch any scales which ping off while you are working.

To test if fish is cooked, pierce the thickest part with a sharp knife; the flesh should be opaque and come away easily from the bone. Fish will continue to cook if left in an oven that has been turned off, so be careful not to overcook it. If fish is overcooked, or kept warm for any length of time, the flesh will soon shrink and dry out.

From left: Spiced goujons of plaice and Sole and prawn roulades (recipes overleaf)

FILLETING FLAT FISH

Flat fish are always delicately flavoured – Dover sole is the most luxurious while lemon sole and plaice are more affordable. Turbot, halibut, brill and dabs are also flat fish and are prepared in the same way. Make stock from the trimmings (see Rich seafood stew, page 52, step 1) for flavouring sauces.

A flexible, ultra-sharp filleting knife is best, otherwise use any long, slender knife.

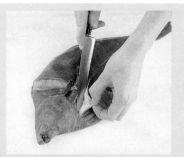

❶ Using scissors, cut off both fins. With fish dark side uppermost, make a cut down the centre (along pale line) with a knife. Make another cut around the head.

❷ Slide the knife under one fish fillet to loosen from the bone. Holding the loosened corner in one hand, slice away the flesh from the bones.

Spiced goujons of plaice

This smart version of fish and chips makes a deliciously simple supper dish to serve to friends with either chips or salad. Prepare in advance up to the deep frying stage.

Serves 4

8 large plaice fillets, skinned
100g/4oz breadcrumbs
1 tsp ground cumin
2 tsp ground paprika
$\frac{1}{4}$ tsp turmeric
seasoning
3 tbsp plain flour
2 eggs, beaten
oil, for deep frying
FOR THE DIP
$\frac{1}{4}$ cucumber, grated
100g/4oz full fat cream cheese
150ml/$\frac{1}{4}$ pint natural yogurt
1 tbsp mayonnaise
lemon slices and parsley, to garnish

❶ Cut the plaice fillets into wide, diagonal strips. Mix together the breadcrumbs, cumin, paprika, turmeric and seasoning. Set aside. Toss fish in the three tablespoons of flour until thoroughly coated; the easiest way is to put flour and fish in a plastic bag and shake.
❷ Dip fish in egg then coat in breadcrumbs. Set aside. Drain cucumber on kitchen paper and mix with cream cheese, yogurt, mayonnaise and seasoning. Transfer to a pretty bowl and set the dip aside.
❸ Heat oil in a deep pan until a piece of bread sizzles when added to it. Fry goujons in batches until pale golden (about 1 minute). Drain on kitchen paper. Garnish with lemon and parsley and serve with the dip.

Sole and prawn roulades

A classic dinner party dish that can be prepared and left in the fridge for an hour or two before your guests arrive. Begin cooking later, but make the evening more enjoyable by doing the preparation in advance. Serve with mangetout peas, carrots and sauté potatoes.

Serves 4

450g/1lb whole prawns
2 tbsp oil
2 celery sticks, chopped
1 bunch spring onions, chopped
seasoning
8 lemon sole fillets, skinned
150ml/$\frac{1}{4}$ pint white wine or fish stock
$5\frac{1}{2}$ tbsp double cream
celery leaves, to garnish

❶ Reserve four prawns. Remove heads of remaining prawns, remove shells and discard. Chop prawn flesh. Fry celery and half of the spring onions in the oil for 1 minute. Add prawns and seasoning. Mix well and remove from heat.
❷ Lay fillets skinned sides up on a board. Spoon stuffing over fillets and pack down lightly.
❸ Roll up fillets and lay, joins facing down to hold them closed, in an ovenproof dish. Pour over the white wine or stock. Cover and bake at 190C/375F/Gas 5 for 25 minutes. Blend juices with remaining spring onions and heat with the cream. Season and pour over roulades. Garnish with celery leaves and reserved prawns.

❸ Continue to slice away the fillet from the bones, keeping your knife close to them. Pull away completely. Cut off the other fillet, turn fish over and repeat on the white side.

❹ To remove any dark patches of flesh on the fish fillets, rub generously with salt. Wash off under cold running water then pat dry with kitchen paper.

❺ To skin fillets, hold firmly by the tail (use a little salt if necessary to get a good grip) and 'saw' knife between skin and flesh, working down length of fillet.

Cod with tartare mayonnaise

Serves 4

Beat together 4 tablespoons mayonnaise, 2 tablespoons single cream or yogurt, 2 tablespoons chopped parsley and add 1 tablespoon each chopped capers and gherkins.

Place four cod steaks on lightly buttered squares of foil. Then spoon over the mayonnaise mixture.

Seal the foil to enclose each piece of fish and bake at 160C/325F/Gas 3 for 25 minutes until the fish flakes easily when it is pierced with a knife.

Serve the cod with some buttered new potatoes in their skins and crisp, fresh lettuce or a mixed salad.

Coley with devilled sauce

Serves 4

Mix 1 tablespoon each Worcestershire sauce, coarse-grain mustard, mango chutney and orange juice. Season. Fry four skinned coley fillets in butter until firm. Turn and spoon over sauce. Cook 1 minute.

Baked trout with bacon

Serves 1

For each serving, place one cleaned and boned trout in a shallow ovenproof dish. Season the trout lightly and tuck several sprigs of fresh tarragon or parsley into the cavity of each piece of fish.

Lay two rashers of smoked bacon in the dish with the trout. Then bake uncovered at 180C/350F/Gas 4 for 25–30 minutes until the fish is completely cooked.

To serve, garnish with some fresh tarragon or parsley.

Tandoori fish

Serves 4

Crush 2 garlic cloves. Mix in a bowl with 4 tablespoons yogurt, 3 tablespoons tomato purée, 2 tablespoons oil, 1 teaspoon ground cumin, $\frac{1}{2}$ teaspoon chilli powder and a good pinch of turmeric.

Season lightly and spoon the mixture over four skinned portions of haddock or cod fillet. Bake at 190C/375F/Gas 5 for 20–25 minutes until the fish flakes easily when it is pierced with a knife.

Serve the tandoori fish on a bed of rice, and garnish with a few wedges of fresh lemon and coriander leaves.

FILLETING ROUND FISH

Round fish include white-fleshed everyday varieties such as haddock, cod and coley or the smaller and richer oily fish such as mackerel, herring, sardines and sprats as well as the delicately-flavoured trout and salmon. If you're lucky enough to be supplied with freshly caught fish or you enjoy experimenting with them in soups and stews, it's well worth knowing how to trim and clean them. Small whole fish such as herring can also be boned effortlessly, ready for stuffing or frying. Here's how to do it with the minimum of fuss.

❶ To remove scales from fish, place on a large sheet of newspaper. Scrape a knife against the skin, working from tail towards head until the scales come away. Use a little salt to get a good grip if necessary.

❷ Using a sharp knife, make a slit along underside of fish down to the vent and scrape out all the innards. Rinse the fish well, inside and out, under cold running water. Carefully cut off head. Trim off all fins with a pair of kitchen scissors.

Grilled stuffed herrings

Serves 4

1 small onion

225g/8oz frozen spinach, thawed

50g/2oz butter

50g/2oz breadcrumbs

2 tbsp grated Parmesan cheese

25g/1oz pine nuts

seasoning

4 small herrings, boned

❶ Peel and chop onion. Place spinach in a sieve and press out liquid. Fry onion in the butter for 2 minutes. Add breadcrumbs, spinach, grated Parmesan cheese, pine nuts and seasoning. Mix well.

❷ Make 4–5 shallow cuts down each side of the fish. Pre-set grill to moderate. Grease a shallow, heatproof dish.

❸ Spoon stuffing into fish; pack down lightly. Dot fish with butter; season. Secure cut edges with cocktail sticks. Transfer to dish and grill for 10 minutes each side, until fish flakes easily.

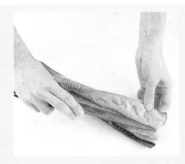

❸ To fillet a round fish, make an incision along the length of the backbone down to the tail. Slide a knife closely along the side of the backbone to release the fillet completely. Repeat on other side. Skin by holding tail firmly and saw knife between skin and flesh, working down length of fillet.

❹ To bone small, whole fish such as herring, continue the cut made on underside down to tail. Open out fish and press down firmly along the backbone with the thumb.

❺ Turn fish over and pull away backbone, pulling away flesh that clings to the bones with the other hand. Snip off backbone at tail end, using scissors.

Left: Grilled stuffed herrings

Rich seafood stew

Serves 4

225g/8oz whole prawns

1 small hake or mullet, filleted and skinned, trimmings reserved

2 carrots, peeled and sliced separately

3 bay leaves

50g/2oz butter

1 leek, sliced

2 celery sticks, sliced

3 garlic cloves

450g/1lb cod, haddock, whiting or coley fillet, skinned

1 tbsp plain flour

seasoning

450g/1lb new potatoes, boiled

150ml/$\frac{1}{4}$ pint double cream

shrimps or prawns, black olives and bay leaves, to garnish

❶ Peel prawns – pull off heads and peel away shells. Place heads and shells in a pan with reserved fish trimmings, a sliced carrot and bay leaves. Add water to cover, bring to the boil, then simmer for 40 minutes.

❷ Melt butter in a flameproof casserole or deep pan. Add remaining carrot, leek, celery and garlic and fry for 3 minutes. Lay filleted fish on top, cover with lid or foil and cook gently for 5 minutes. Remove fish. Stir flour into vegetables.

❸ Strain fish stock through a sieve into pan. Bring to the boil, stirring. Season, then add potatoes and cream. Heat through. Add fish and cook for a further minute. Serve with garnishes.

Monkfish parcels with pepper sauce

Serves 4

675–750g/1½–1¾lb monkfish tail

50g/2oz Parmesan, coarsely grated

4 streaky bacon rashers

FOR THE SAUCE

1 tbsp olive oil

2 red peppers, seeded and chopped

225g/8oz can chopped tomatoes

½ tsp chilli powder

seasoning

❶ Preheat the oven to 180C/ 350F/Gas 4. Cut through monkfish on both sides of the bone to remove the fillets. Halve each one and place between two pieces of damp greaseproof paper. Beat with a rolling pin to flatten slightly. Using a sharp knife, cut a small pocket along the side of each fillet.
❷ Tuck the Parmesan into the pockets. Stretch the bacon rashers and cut them in half. Use two halves crossways to wrap each piece of fish into a parcel, tucking the ends underneath. Place in a lightly greased ovenproof dish and bake for 25 minutes.
❸ To make the sauce, heat the oil and add peppers, tomatoes, chilli powder and seasoning with four tablespoons of water. Bring to the boil, cover and simmer for 10 minutes until peppers are soft.
❹ Place the monkfish parcels on serving plates and spoon the sauce around them.

Peppered salmon fillets in cream

Serves 4

2 tsp mixed peppercorns, finely crushed

4 salmon fillets

2 tbsp olive oil

1 glass white wine

6 tbsp double cream

salt

❶ Sprinkle the crushed peppercorns evenly over both sides of the salmon fillets, then lightly press into the fish.
❷ Heat the oil in a frying pan and cook the fillets over a low heat for 4 minutes. Turn them over and fry for a further 2–3 minutes until just cooked through.
❸ Drain the fish; keep warm. Add the wine to the pan and boil rapidly until it reduces slightly. Pour in cream and bring to the boil. Add salt, then spoon sauce over fish.

Smoked haddock and cream tart

Serves 6

FOR THE PASTRY

75g/3oz cream cheese

75g/3oz lightly salted butter, slightly softened

100g/4oz plain flour

beaten egg, to glaze

FOR THE FILLING

450g/1lb smoked haddock fillet

4 tbsp milk

seasoning

2 red onions, cut into fine rings

1 tsp olive oil

1 egg

120ml/4fl oz double cream

8 fresh basil leaves, shredded

❶ Preheat the oven to 200C/ 400F/Gas 6. Beat together the cream cheese and butter, then gradually work in the flour. Mix into a dough and chill for 15 minutes.
❷ Roll out the dough to a 23cm/9in round and transfer to a greased baking sheet. Brush the edges with beaten egg, then fold them in to create a small wall. Chill.
❸ To make the filling, place the haddock in a pan with the milk and seasoning. Cover and simmer gently for 6–8 minutes until just cooked through. Drain, reserving milk. Flake the fish, discarding any skin and remaining bones.
❹ Fry the onion rings in the olive oil for 2 minutes until softened. Arrange in the pastry case with the flaked haddock.
❺ Strain the reserved milk and beat in the egg, cream and seasoning. Pour on top of the filling. Tuck the shredded basil leaves around the fish. Bake for 20–25 minutes until the pastry is golden and the custard is just firm. Serve warm with a mixed salad.

Fish steaks en papillotte

Serves 4

1 tbsp olive oil

½ small onion, chopped

225g/8oz frozen leaf spinach, thawed and squeezed to remove excess water

25g/1oz pine nuts

25g/1oz Parmesan, grated

15g/½oz butter

4 cod or haddock steaks, cut from thickest part of the fish, boned

seasoning

❶ Preheat the oven to 190C/ 375F/Gas 5. Heat the oil in a small pan and fry the onion for 2 minutes. Stir in the spinach, pine nuts, Parmesan and seasoning; warm through and remove from the heat.

❷ Cut four rounds of greaseproof paper, about 25cm/10in diameter, and spread half of the butter over one side of each. Lay the fish steaks on top and pack the spinach mixture into the cavities.

❸ Dot the fish with the remaining butter and season lightly. Pull the greaseproof paper over the steaks, folding and rolling the edges together to seal. Place on a baking sheet and cook in the oven for 25 minutes. Serve in the paper parcels.

Skewered squid and prawns with lime dressing

Serves 4 as a starter

350g/12oz prepared squid

juice of 1 lime

1 tbsp clear honey

2 tbsp olive oil

8 whole peeled prawns

seasoning

lime wedges and a few flat-leaf parsley sprigs, to garnish

FOR THE DRESSING

3 limes

6 tbsp olive oil

1 tbsp golden caster sugar

❶ Cut the squid into 5mm/$\frac{1}{4}$in wide rings. Mix with lime juice, honey and oil, cover and marinate for 6 hours or overnight.

❷ To make the dressing, peel the limes and cut between the membranes to release the segments. Blend in a food processor, gradually add the oil and whizz until the mixture thickens. Transfer to a pan, add the sugar and dissolve over a gentle heat.

❸ Drain the squid on kitchen paper and thread alternately with the prawns on to four wooden skewers. Season and grill for 3–4 minutes until golden. Reheat dressing and serve with the kebabs. Garnish with the lime wedges and parsley sprigs.

Below: Fish steaks en papillotte

Grey mullet with cheese

Serves 2

2 × 175g/6oz grey mullet fillets
seasoning
1 tsp wholegrain mustard
4 tbsp double cream
75g/3oz Gruyère cheese, grated
25g/1oz fresh wholemeal
breadcrumbs
2 tbsp snipped fresh chives

❶ Preheat the oven to 180C/
350F/Gas 4. Lay the fillets in a
shallow, oiled baking dish and
season them. Mix mustard and
double cream together and pour
over to cover the fish.
❷ Mix together the cheese,
breadcrumbs and chives. Sprinkle
the cheese mixture over the fish.
Bake uncovered for about
15–20 minutes until the topping is
crispy and golden and the fish is
cooked through.

Parrot fish with julienne of vegetables

Serves 2

350g/12oz parrot fish fillets, cut
into diagonal slices
2 small carrots, cut into
matchsticks
2 courgettes, cut into
matchsticks
100g/4oz fine green beans
seasoning
50g/2oz Coriander and lime
butter (see page 63)

❶ Place the fish and the
vegetables in a steamer, season
and steam for 10–12 minutes.
Serve fish with the vegetables as a
garnish and accompany with the
Coriander and lime butter.

Red snapper with tomato sauce

Serves 4

2 garlic cloves, crushed
1 small onion, finely chopped
2 tbsp olive oil
750g/1½lb tomatoes, skinned,
seeded and chopped
1 tsp tomato purée
4 tbsp chopped fresh parsley
grated rind of 1 lemon
seasoning
4 red snappers, about 225g/8oz
each

❶ Preheat the oven to 190C/
375F/ Gas 5. Soften the garlic and
onion in the oil. Add the tomatoes,
purée, parsley and lemon rind.
Cook for 10 minutes, stirring, until
slightly reduced.
❷ Season inside the fish and
place in an oiled baking dish. Pour
the sauce around them and bake
for about 25 minutes. Serve hot.

Pan-fried halibut with leeks

Serves 2

2 tbsp olive oil

15g/½oz unsalted butter

4 small leeks, sliced

2 × 200g/7oz halibut steaks

seasoning

2 tbsp vermouth

❶ In a large frying pan heat 1 tablespoon of the oil with the butter until sizzling. Add the leeks and cook over a medium heat until soft. Push them to one side of the pan, add the remaining oil and fry the halibut steaks for about 6 minutes on each side until golden. Season each side as they cook.

❷ Sprinkle over the vermouth, cover the pan with a lid and cook for a few minutes more.

Flaked trout with pasta

Serves 4

225g/8oz pasta shells

3 trout fillets

seasoning

1 small Ogen or Galia melon, halved and seeded

½ bunch spring onions, trimmed and chopped

50g/2oz pistachio nuts, shelled and skinned

25g/1oz stem ginger, finely diced

4 tbsp mayonnaise

2 tbsp single cream

3 tbsp chopped fresh parsley

❶ Bring a pan of salted water to the boil, add the pasta, then cover and cook until just firm to bite. Drain and leave to cool.

❷ Place the trout fillets in a pan with 2 tablespoons of water. Season lightly, cover and steam for 8 minutes until cooked through. Cool slightly, then flake the trout, discarding skin and any bones. Set aside.

❸ Using a melon baller, scoop the melon flesh into a bowl with any juice. Add the spring onions, half of the pistachios, the stem ginger, pasta and flaked trout.

❹ Mix together the mayonnaise, cream and parsley. Add to the bowl, season to taste and toss lightly. Serve at once, sprinkled with the remaining pistachios.

From left: Grey mullet with cheese, Parrot fish with julienne of vegetables, Red snapper with tomato sauce and Pan-fried halibut with leeks

Braised tuna steaks

You can also braise other large oily fish, such as bonito and swordfish, which are sold as steaks ready for grilling, although braising helps the fish retain more moisture.

Serves 2

2 tbsp olive oil

2 × 175–225g/6–8oz tuna steaks

1 small onion, very finely chopped

1 carrot, finely sliced

1 celery stick, finely sliced

2 beefsteak tomatoes, skinned, seeded and roughly chopped

1 tbsp fresh thyme leaves, plus extra to garnish

$5\frac{1}{2}$ tbsp dry white wine

seasoning

❶ Heat the oil over a high heat in a shallow, flameproof casserole and quickly fry the tuna until lightly browned on each side. Remove from the casserole and set aside.
❷ Reduce the heat slightly, add the onion, carrot and celery and fry for a few minutes until softened. Stir in the tomatoes and thyme leaves and cook for about 5 minutes until the tomatoes have softened. Preheat the oven to 160C/325F/ Gas 3.
❸ Lay the tuna steaks on top of the cooked vegetables, pour over the white wine, add seasoning and cover. Bake for 40–50 minutes until tender. Garnish with thyme.

Grilled fish steaks with orange and caper butter

Serves 4

2 oranges

4 small shark or swordfish steaks

50g/2oz butter

2 tsp chopped fresh rosemary

2 tsp chopped fresh parsley

1 tbsp capers, chopped

seasoning

fresh rosemary sprigs, to garnish

❶ Pour the juice of one orange over the steaks and marinate for at least 1 hour. Meanwhile, finely grate the rind of the other orange and squeeze out the juice.
❷ Melt the butter in a pan, add the orange rind and juice with the herbs, capers and seasoning and heat through for 1 minute.
❸ Drain the steaks and grill for 6 minutes on each side or until cooked through. Pour over the sauce and garnish with rosemary.

Baked anchovy pie

Serves 3–4

225g/8oz potatoes, thinly sliced

225g/8oz turnips, thinly sliced

225g/8oz celeriac, thinly sliced

1 large onion, sliced

50g/2oz can anchovy fillets, drained

150ml/$\frac{1}{4}$ pint double cream

150ml/$\frac{1}{4}$ pint fish stock

seasoning

❶ Preheat the oven to 180C/ 350F/Gas 4. Layer half of potatoes, turnips and celeriac with onions in a shallow ovenproof dish. Arrange anchovies on top, then cover with layers of remaining vegetables.
❷ Beat together the cream, stock and seasoning and pour over the pie. Bake for 1 hour until golden.

Squid with garlic and parsley

Halve these quantities for a delightfully light dish to serve as a starter.

Serves 4

450g/1lb small, prepared squid

2 tbsp olive oil

3 garlic cloves, crushed

6 tbsp chopped fresh parsley, plus extra to garnish

a little lemon juice

seasoning

❶ Slice the squid bodies, but leave the tentacles whole. Blanch the squid in boiling water for 2 minutes, then drain.
❷ Heat the oil in a small frying pan and fry the squid, garlic and parsley for 3–4 minutes. Sprinkle over the lemon juice and add seasoning to taste. Cool and serve chilled. Garnish with finely chopped parsley.

Court bouillon

Fish can be poached or steamed in water, but the flavour is greatly enhanced by poaching or steaming whole fish, steaks and fillets in this vegetable-based liquid. Make this with a good dry but fruity flavoured white wine.

Makes 900ml/1$\frac{1}{2}$ pints

1 small onion, sliced

1 carrot, sliced

1 celery stick, sliced

4 peppercorns

good pinch of salt

1 bay leaf

few parsley stalks, crushed

knob of butter

300ml/$\frac{1}{2}$ pint dry white wine

❶ Place all the ingredients, except for the wine, together with 600ml/

1 pint of water in a pan and bring to the boil. Cover and simmer for 15 minutes, add the wine and simmer for a further 15 minutes. Leave to cool, then strain the liquid and use as required.

Red pepper butter

Makes about 100g/4oz

1 small red pepper, seeded and diced

100g/4oz unsalted butter

freshly ground black pepper

❶ Place the pepper in a blender or food processor and whizz for a few seconds, then add the butter, grind in some black pepper and whizz again until all the ingredients are thoroughly mixed.

❷ Spoon out the butter on to a piece of greaseproof paper and form into a fat roll, then wrap in the greaseproof paper and chill in the fridge until required. To serve, cut thin slices from the chilled roll.

Rouille

Serves 4–6

3 garlic cloves, chopped

1 red pepper, seeded and chopped

1 fresh red chilli, seeded and chopped

4 slices stale bread, soaked in water, then squeezed out

3 tbsp olive oil

❶ Place all the ingredients in a blender or food processor and whizz until thoroughly blended. Or you can crush the ingredients to a paste, using a large mortar and pestle.

Coriander and lime butter

You can vary the flavour of this butter with different herbs and fruits while using the same method. Ring the changes by trying rosemary or tarragon with orange, or parsley or thyme with lemon.

Makes about 100g/4oz

100g/4oz unsalted butter

chopped fresh coriander leaves

grated rind of 1 lime

2 tsp green peppercorns, crushed

❶ Mix together the butter, coriander, lime rind and peppercorns. Place on greaseproof paper and form into a roll; wrap and chill until firm. When ready to serve, cut into slices.

Anchovy and olive butter

Makes about 100g/4oz

6–8 anchovy fillets

100g/4oz unsalted butter, softened

2 tsp olive paste

❶ Place the anchovy fillets, softened butter and olive paste in a medium-sized bowl. Beat all the ingredients together thoroughly. Chill in the fridge until required.

From left: Braised tuna steaks and Squid with garlic and parsley

Shellfish

Our step-by-step instructions will really help in the preparation of shellfish, so buy fresh mussels, clams, shrimps and prawns from your fishmonger if you possibly can and eat them on the day of purchase.

Mouclade of mussels

Serves 6 as a starter, 4 as a main course

25g/1oz butter
1 small onion, sliced
1 small head of fennel, sliced
2 garlic cloves, crushed
2 tbsp chopped parsley or fennel
1 glass white wine
2 tbsp Pernod (optional)
1.75kg/4lb mussels, cleaned
6 tbsp double cream
seasoning
fennel or samphire, to garnish

❶ Melt the butter in a large pan. Add the onion, fennel and garlic and fry gently until softened.
❷ Stir in herbs, wine and Pernod, if using, and bring to the boil. Add mussels, cover with the lid and cook as on page 67, step 3.
❸ Drain the mussels and keep warm. Stir cream and seasoning into pan juices and heat through.
❹ Pour sauce over mussels, garnish with fennel or samphire. Serve with plenty of warm bread to mop up the juices.

Baked scallops in their shells

Serves 6
450g/1lb potatoes
225g/8oz celeriac
50g/2oz butter
3 tbsp chopped parsley or chervil
a little milk
12 scallops, cleaned
100g/4oz button mushrooms, halved
1 tsp cornflour
150ml/$\frac{1}{4}$ pint double cream
seasoning
25g/1oz finely grated Cheddar
seasoning
sprig of parsley or chervil, to garnish

❶ Preheat the oven to 190C/375F/Gas 5. Peel potatoes and celeriac and cut into small chunks. Cook in boiling, salted water for about 15 minutes until tender. Drain and mash with half of the butter, herbs and milk.
❷ Place in a piping bag fitted with a large star nozzle. Pipe shells around edges of six scallop shells or small ovenproof dishes.
❸ Cut orange coral from each scallop. Cut white flesh in half.
❹ Melt remaining butter in a frying pan. Add mushrooms and white part of scallops and fry gently for 1 minute. Stir in scallop corals and spoon mixture into shells.
❺ Blend cornflour with juices left in pan. Add cream and seasoning and cook, stirring until thickened. Spoon over scallops.
❻ Sprinkle with cheese and bake for 20 minutes or until turning golden. Serve garnished with parsley or chervil.

From left: Mouclade of mussels and Baked scallops in their shells

BIVALVES

Bivalves are molluscs which inhabit a hinged double shell. Fresh mussels and clams are always bought live, and scrubbed and cooked as in steps 1–3. Cockles are rarely seen in shells as they are prepared and cooked at the sea fisheries. Oysters should be bought live with the shells closed or closing when tapped and they should feel quite heavy as they should be full of water. Scallops usually come ready cleaned but they are easy to prepare if not.

❶ Place mussels in a bowl, cover with cold water and sprinkle with oatmeal. This is done to clean out and feed the mussels. Refrigerate or keep in a cool place until ready to use.

❷ Scrub with a brush or abrasive cloth and scrape away any barnacles with a knife. Pull away the 'beard', the tuft in the hinge. Wash, discarding any damaged mussels or any that remain open when tapped.

Clam chowder

Serves 4 *Quick & Tasty*

Cook 12 large clams (see steps 1–3 above) and remove from shells. Fry one chopped onion and four streaky bacon rashers in 25g/1oz melted butter. Add 400g/14oz can chopped tomatoes, $\frac{1}{2}$ teaspoon of sugar, 150ml/$\frac{1}{4}$ pint stock, one large chopped potato, $\frac{1}{2}$ teaspoon of curry powder and the clams. Bring to boil, simmer until potatoes are tender. Stir in 4 tablespoons cream; season. Heat gently. Garnish with cream, paprika and parsley.

Cockles with pasta

Serves 4 *Quick & Tasty*

Fry one chopped onion, two crushed garlic cloves and one chopped celery stick in 3 tablespoons of olive oil until softened. Add 400g/14oz can chopped tomatoes, 1 tablespoon of tomato purée, $\frac{1}{2}$ teaspoon of sugar and a sprinkling of mixed herbs. Simmer until pulpy. Add 225g/8oz cooked spaghetti and 350g/12oz cockles; cleaned (see steps 1–2 above). Heat for 1–2 minutes and season. Serve with Parmesan.

Potted shrimps

Serves 2–4 *Quick & Tasty*

Peel 225g/8oz cooked whole pink or brown shrimps. Melt 50g/2oz butter with a pinch of cayenne pepper and nutmeg, and stir in the shrimps. Pack them into ramekins

Left: Clam chowder

3 To cook mussels, tip into a pan with a little water, white wine or stock. Cover immediately with a tight-fitting lid and cook for 3–5 minutes, shaking the pan until they open. Discard any which do not open.

4 To open oysters, insert a strong knife between the shells next to the hinge. Twist the knife until the hinge breaks. Sever muscle from shell, retaining juices. Serve in a half shell with lemon juice and cayenne.

5 To prepare scallops, slide a thin knife between the shells and twist apart, cutting the muscle away from the shell. Discard the flat shell. Pull off greyish skin and cut away the black sac. Rinse well.

or other individual serving dishes and chill in the fridge for several hours until firm. Loosen around the edges with a knife, then turn out and serve with toast or bread. This starter can be made in advance in the morning for the evening.

Seafood salad

Serves 4

Scrub and cook 450g/1lb new potatoes. Peel 450g/1lb cooked prawns. Slice one leek and fry in 3 tablespoons of olive oil. Add 1 tablespoon of lemon juice and 225g/8oz cleaned mussels and cover with a lid. Cook until mussels open (see steps 1–3 above). Arrange potatoes, leeks, mussels, prawns, 100g/4oz cockles and watercress sprigs on plates. Season the pan juices and pour over salad. Serve at once, garnished with fresh herbs.

Right: Seafood salad

PRAWNS AND SHRIMPS

Prawns and shrimps vary in size and colour and most have been frozen, so they should not be re-frozen unless cooked.

Choose unshelled prawns and peel them yourself as ready-peeled ones can taste watery. Ready-cooked prawns can be served cold with mayonnaise, fried or steamed or peeled and added to sauces. Uncooked prawns are delicious fried or grilled with butter until they turn pink.

❶ In order to peel a cooked prawn or shrimp, you must first pinch off the head and then carefully peel away the papery, delicate shell, leaving the tip of the tail on it if you so desire.

❷ To cook raw prawns, remove heads if you like, then heat a little butter and olive oil with crushed garlic in a frying pan. Add prawns and cook for 1–3 minutes on each side, depending on size, until pink.

Luxurious prawn salad

Serves 4
FOR THE HERB MAYONNAISE
4 tbsp mayonnaise
2 tsp wholegrain mustard
2 tsp white wine vinegar
$\frac{1}{2}$ tsp tomato purée
3 tbsp double cream
$\frac{1}{2}$ tsp caster sugar
2–3 tbsp chopped fresh herbs (eg tarragon, fennel, dill, parsley)
seasoning

FOR THE SALAD
frisée, cherry tomatoes and oyster or button mushrooms
450g/1lb whole cooked prawns, peeled (see steps 1–3 above)
handful of whole cooked pink or brown shrimps
4 cooked king prawns, to garnish
sprigs of parsley or tarragon, to garnish

❶ Mix together the mayonnaise, mustard, vinegar, tomato purée, cream, sugar, herbs and seasoning.

❷ Arrange the lettuce, tomatoes and mushrooms attractively on serving plates. Add prawns and shrimps. Garnish with the king prawns and herbs and serve with the herb mayonnaise.

From left: Luxurious prawn salad with herb mayonnaise and Grilled skewered prawns

❸ It is important to remove the dark intestinal vein from large prawns. Peel them first, then make a shallow cut along the back through to the vein. Rinse under running water to remove vein.

❹ Save all prawn trimmings, as well as any lobster and crab trimmings, for stock. Place in a pan with bay leaves, peppercorns, celery and herbs. Cover with water and bring slowly to the boil.

❺ Reduce heat and simmer gently for 30–40 minutes. Leave to cool slightly, then strain through a sieve. The stock can be frozen and used for seafood sauces, soups or stews.

Grilled skewered prawns

Serves 4

4 streaky bacon rashers
8 cooked king prawns
225g/8oz cooked whole prawns
2 garlic cloves, crushed
1 tbsp chopped fresh parsley, dill or fennel
50g/2oz butter
bay leaves and sprigs of dill or fennel, to garnish
mayonnaise or Herb mayonnaise (see opposite page), to serve

❶ Remove rind from bacon rashers and stretch with the back of a knife. Halve each slice.
❷ Peel king prawns (see steps 1 and 3 above), reserving tails for decoration. Peel small prawns.
❸ Put a skewer through the thick end, then through the tail end, of a king prawn. Push reserved tail between prawn and skewer to decorate.

❹ Thread small prawns, two bacon pieces and another king prawn on to skewer, then thread three more skewers in the same way. Place on grill rack. Mix garlic, herbs and butter together and brush over kebabs.
❺ Cook for 2 minutes on each side. Garnish with herbs. Serve with mayonnaise.

Poultry

A versatile base for all kinds of flavours, why not indulge in a spectacular roast or galantine for that special occasion.

Summer roast turkey

Serves 8
50g/2oz butter or oil
1 large onion, chopped
1 bunch watercress, chopped
grated rind of 1 orange
1 egg
100g/4oz ground almonds
100g/4oz breadcrumbs
seasoning
2.75kg/6lb oven-ready turkey, giblets removed
FOR THE GLAZE
50g/2oz butter, melted
grated rind of 1 orange
3 tbsp clear honey
orange slices, watercress and parsley, to garnish

❶ Melt butter or oil and fry onion until softened. Combine watercress, onion, rind, egg, almonds, breadcrumbs and seasoning.

❷ Turn the turkey on to its breast and spoon as much stuffing into the neck cavity as it will comfortably take. Secure the flap of skin over the stuffing with cocktail sticks. (Any extra stuffing can be packed into a tin or ovenproof dish and baked until firm).

❸ Preheat the oven to 180C/350F/Gas 4. Truss the turkey and place in roasting tin. Mix together the melted butter, orange rind and honey and brush over the skin. Cook for $2\frac{1}{2}$–$2\frac{3}{4}$ hours or until the juices run clear. Cover turkey breast with foil if it starts to over-brown.

❹ Cover loosely with foil and leave to rest in a warm place for 15 minutes before carving. Garnish with orange slices, watercress and parsley.

From left: Summer roast turkey and Roast duck with raspberries (recipe overleaf)

ROASTING

Stuffing can be made in advance, but stuff the bird only just before cooking (and always in the neck cavity, never the body).

Thorough cooking is essential. For a chicken or turkey up to 3.5kg/8lb, allow 20 minutes per 450g/1lb plus 20 minutes at 180C/350F/Gas 4. Turkeys over 3.5kg/8lb, allow 15 minutes per 450g/1lb. Duck needs 20 minutes per 450g/1lb at 200C/400F/Gas 6. To test if the bird is cooked, pierce the thigh – the juices should run clear. If not, cook for 10 minutes and test again.

❸ To complete the trussing, wrap a piece of the string around the parson's nose and then loop it around the bird's legs. Pull the string tightly and tie it in a knot.

❶ After cleaning, inside and out, pat the bird dry, trim drumstick bones and cut off wing tips. For extra flavour, place garlic, an onion or fresh herbs inside body cavity.

❹ Grease chicken and turkey with butter to keep it moist during cooking. Mix the butter with finely chopped fresh herbs if you wish before spreading it over the skin.

❷ To truss chicken or turkey, place a length of fine string under the bird and secure around wing bones. Bring the string over the legs towards the front of the bird.

❺ Before you roast duck, always prick the skin, except the top of the breast, with a fork. All poultry can be cooked on a rack placed over roasting tin – use juices for gravy.

Roast duck with raspberries

Serves 4

2.25–2.75g/5–6 lb oven-ready duck, thawed, if frozen
$\frac{1}{2}$ tsp Chinese five spice powder
225g/8oz raspberries
3 tbsp raspberry or red wine vinegar
3 tbsp dark muscovado sugar
seasoning
celery leaves, raspberries and star anise (optional), to garnish

❶ Preheat the oven to 200C/ 400F/Gas 6. Place the duck on a roasting rack and rub the five spice powder all over the skin. Allow 20 minutes cooking time per 450g/1lb.
❷ Place raspberries in a small pan with the vinegar, sugar and a little seasoning. Cook gently for about 5 minutes until pulpy, then press through a nylon sieve into a pan.
❸ When the duck is cooked through, transfer to a serving plate and keep warm. Strain the fat from the roasting tin, add any remaining juices to the raspberry sauce and bring slowly to the boil.
❹ Garnish the duck with celery leaves, raspberries and star anise and serve with the sauce.

Gingered duck

Serves 2

Mix juice of one lime with 2.5 cm/1 in piece chopped ginger, one chopped chilli, four sliced spring onions and two crushed garlic cloves. Spoon over two duck breasts and leave for 2 hours. Drain duck and score skin. Fry in oil for 15 minutes.
Drain off fat. Add marinade juices, 2 tablespoons brown sugar, seasoning and $5\frac{1}{2}$ tbsp water. Cover, simmer for 10 minutes.

Crispy chicken wings

Serves 4

Mix 3 tablespoons clear honey, 1 tablespoon soy sauce, 2 teaspoons five spice powder, 2 tablespoons ketchup and one crushed garlic clove. Brush over 8–10 chicken wings and grill for 15 minutes.

Spicy chicken

Serves 4

Crush $\frac{1}{4}$ cinnamon stick, 2 teaspoons cardamom pods, 1 teaspoon fennel seed, 2 teaspoons coriander seeds, $\frac{1}{4}$ teaspoon chillies. Add 1 tablespoon sesame seeds and salt. Coat 450g/1lb boned, cubed chicken. Fry one sliced onion. Add chicken and cook 8 minutes.

Peppered turkey steaks

Serves 4

Crush 2 tablespoon peppercorns. Mix with salt and use to coat 750g/1$\frac{1}{2}$lb turkey fillets. Fry in 15g/$\frac{1}{2}$oz butter and 2 tablespoons of oil for 2 minutes each side.

Chicken parcels

Serves 2

For each serving, wrap two small slices of Cheddar around two boned chicken thighs. Stretch two rindless rashers of streaky bacon, using the back of a knife. Wrap a rasher around each parcel and tie loosely.

Brush chicken parcels lightly with oil and bake at 190C/375F/ Gas 5 for 25 minutes until the bacon is crisp and brown.

Below: Chicken parcels

JOINTING

Chicken, turkey and duck portions can be expensive, so it's well worth learning the simple technique of jointing whole birds, particularly if you're feeding a crowd. There are several methods – the one shown here is useful for chickens, small turkeys and duck, and it simply, requires a medium-sized knife and a sturdy chopping board.

Work carefully, cutting as much flesh as you can from the carcase to get eight equal-sized pieces to cook. Use bones to make a stock.

❶ Hold the bird firmly in one hand with the breast uppermost. Cut through the skin between the leg and the breast, using a sharp knife.

❷ Twist leg and pull away from body, then use a knife to release thigh bone. Cut away leg completely, taking as much meat from carcase as possible. Repeat other side.

Chicken in red wine

Serves 4

25g/1oz butter
2 tbsp oil
12 button onions
100g/4oz button mushrooms
2 tbsp flour
seasoning
1.5kg/3lb chicken, jointed (see steps above)
4 rashers smoked back bacon
3 garlic cloves, crushed
$\frac{1}{2}$ bottle red wine
150ml/$\frac{1}{4}$ pint chicken stock
2 tbsp chopped fresh parsley
sprigs of fresh parsley, to garnish

❶ Melt the butter with the oil in a frying pan. Add onions and fry for 3–4 minutes until golden. Add the mushrooms and fry for a further minute. Remove from the heat, drain and reserve on a plate.
❷ Sprinkle flour on a plate and season lightly. Use to generously coat the chicken pieces.

❸ Add a little more oil to pan if it is necessary and fry chicken quickly on both sides. Add chopped bacon and garlic and cook for 1 minute.
❹ Stir in wine, stock and seasoning. Add parsley and transfer to ovenproof dish. Cook at 180C/350F/Gas 4 for 1 hour until tender, adding onions and mushrooms after 30 minutes. Garnish with parsley.

From left: Chicken in red wine and Garlicky Mediterranean casserole

3 Make a diagonal cut about three-quarters of the way down the bird's breast to the wing joint. Cut through the joint and remove wing, taking a little of the breast.

4 Cut down the centre of the breast through to the breastbone. Scrape away the meat from the carcase to remove one side of the breast. Repeat other side.

5 Cut each breast in half crossways. Place legs, skin side down, and cut through the fat to detach drumsticks from thighs. You can pull away the skin and discard it.

Garlicky Mediterranean casserole

Serves 4

1 yellow pepper

1 orange or red pepper

1 head of garlic

4 tbsp olive oil

1 large onion, sliced

1.5kg/3lb chicken, jointed (see steps above)

400g/14oz can tomatoes

1 tsp caster sugar

2 tbsp chopped fresh basil, or 1 tsp dried

seasoning

black olives and fresh basil or parsley sprigs, to garnish

1 Seed peppers and cut into chunks. Separate garlic cloves, discarding outer layers of skin.
2 Heat oil in a frying pan. Add onion and garlic and fry gently for 5 minutes. Remove from pan with a slotted spoon. Add chicken to pan, skin sides down, and fry until golden all over.

3 Mix onion, peppers, tomatoes, sugar, basil and seasoning in a large ovenproof dish. Add chicken pieces and tuck in garlic.
4 Cover and bake in a preheated oven at 180C/350F/Gas 4 for 1 hour until tender. Serve garnished with olives and herbs.

BONING

For a special occasion, a partially boned and stuffed chicken, turkey or duck looks very professional indeed, and it carves easily into neat slices of both meat and stuffing to make a delicious combination of textures. Prepare the chicken a day in advance – which means cooking it even if you're serving it cold.

The chicken bones should be browned in the oven and simmered with onion, celery and carrots to make a delicious stock for those who like gravy.

❸ Cut through the wing joint. Bone the other side of the chicken in the same way, scraping away as much meat as possible from the bird's carcase.

❶ Remove tips from wings and first bone section. Lay breast down, cut along centre of back then, down one side, scrape meat from backbone and ribcage.

❹ Trim the chicken meat away from the breastbone and then remove the carcase. Carefully cut away and discard any visible sinews and fat.

❷ Press the knife into the thigh joint. Cut and twist to release the bone, then continue scraping away meat from carcase until the breastbone is exposed.

❺ Cut along thighs to expose bone. Cut through joint, scrape away meat to release thigh bone, leaving drumsticks intact. Scrape meat from wing bones and pull out.

Galantine of chicken

Serves 8–10

750g/1½lb piece smoked hock or collar gammon

1 bunch spring onions, finely chopped

1 red pepper, seeded and finely chopped

450g/1lb herby or pork sausagemeat

1 tbsp paprika

2 tbsp chopped fresh parsley or coriander

seasoning

1.75–2.25kg/4–5lb chicken, boned (see left)

75g/3oz butter

sprigs of flatfleaf parsley or coriander, to garnish

❶ Soak gammon in cold water for 2 hours, then drain. Weigh gammon and calculate cooking time at 25 minutes per 450g/1lb, plus an extra 25 minutes. Place in a large pan, cover with cold water and bring to the boil. Skim surface, reduce heat and cover. Boil for calculated time, then leave to cool in the cooking liquid. Lift out and trim off the rind and fat.

❷ Mix together the chopped spring onions, red pepper, sausagemeat, paprika, fresh parsley or coriander and season well with salt and freshly ground pepper.

❸ Lay boned chicken on board, skin side down. Spoon half the stuffing down the centre. Place gammon over stuffing. Use remaining stuffing to enclose gammon.

❹ Bring chicken up over stuffing. Thread a trussing needle or darning needle with string.

❺ Sew up chicken, gathering in skin at the ends. Knot the string then turn over chicken so the join is underneath.

❻ Take another length of string and slide it under the chicken. Bring ends up between legs and breast. Loop ends around legs and tie them tightly together.

❼ Weigh the chicken and calculate the cooking time, allowing 15 minutes per 450g/1lb. Place in a roasting tin. Melt butter and use to soak a double thickness of muslin, about 30cm/12in square. Lay the buttered muslin over the chicken to keep it moist.

❽ Bake in a preheated oven at 180C/350F/Gas 4 for the calculated cooking time. To test whether it's cooked, pierce a thigh with a skewer – the juices should run clear. If not, return to the oven.

❾ Leave the cooked chicken to stand for 15 minutes before you carve it. Alternatively, cool and chill in the fridge if serving it cold. Remove the string by giving one end a fairly firm tug, it should come away in a single piece. Serve the galantine of chicken on a large plate with sprigs of flatleaf parsley or fresh coriander.

Below: Galantine of chicken

Meat

*Make the most of meat with a
traditional roast or pot roast, or try
one of our 'quick and tasty'
variations for something different.*

Spiced pork with crackling

Serves 8

1 onion, chopped
225g/8oz good-quality pork
sausagemeat
½ tsp ground turmeric
1 tsp each of coarsely crushed
fennel seeds, cumin, coriander
¼ tsp chilli powder
2 tbsp finely chopped fresh
coriander leaves
seasoning
1.5–1.75kg/3½–4lb spare rib of
pork, boned and finely scored

❶ Mix together onion,
sausagemeat, spices and
coriander. Season lightly. Pack
meat with stuffing. Roll and tie at
2.5cm/1in intervals.
❷ Weigh meat. Rub a little salt into
thoroughly scored skin and place
in roasting tin. Roast, following
chart (page 81).

❸ Extra sausagemeat stuffing can
be rolled into balls and baked
round meat for the final
45 minutes. Make gravy as in
Roasts, step 5 overleaf.

Lamb ballotine

Serves 6–8

1 onion, chopped
350g/12oz courgettes, finely
grated and squeezed of excess
moisture
75g/3oz salted cashews or
almonds, chopped
50g/2oz breadcrumbs
¼ tsp grated nutmeg
seasoning
1.5–1.75kg/3½–4lb lamb shoulder,
boned
2 tbsp redcurrant jelly (see page
184).

❶ Mix together onion, courgettes,
nuts, breadcrumbs and nutmeg
and lightly season. Pack lamb with

stuffing (if necessary, cut a deeper
cavity with a sharp knife) and tie up
ends of the meat with trussing
needle and fine string.
❷ With neat side uppermost, use
lengths of string to tie lamb into a
domed 'ball'. Weigh meat and
roast, following chart (page 81).
Drain, transfer to a serving plate
and make the gravy as in Roasts,
step 5 overleaf, adding the
redcurrant jelly to juices.

**From left: Spiced pork with crackling
and Lamb ballotine**

ROASTS

A classic roast makes a foolproof choice for any occasion. For best results, use beef sirloin, fore or wing rib; lamb leg, loin, saddle (double loin), best end, shoulder; pork leg, loin, spare rib, hand and spring. If you lack confidence when carving, choose a boned and rolled joint which is easy to slice. Ask the butcher for the bones to make a well-flavoured gravy. Brown the bones in a hot oven, then simmer in water with an unpeeled onion, carrot and celery stick for 2–3 hours. Strain the liquid.

❶ Preheat the oven to 220C/ 425F/Gas 7. Weigh the stuffed, rolled or 'bone in' joint and calculate cooking time (see roasting chart below right). Wipe the meat and place in roasting tin.

❷ For added flavour lay joint, fatty side up, on a bed of garlic, onion or celery. Beef can be spread with coarse mustard; lamb spiked with slivers of garlic and sprigs of herbs, such as rosemary.

Skewered bacon with dill and mustard dressing

Serves 4 *Quick & Tasty*

Soak 175g/6oz prunes for several hours, then drain. Beat together 150ml/¼ pint soured cream, 4 teaspoons of coarse mustard, 1 tablespoon of mayonnaise, 1 tablespoon of chopped dill and seasoning. Slice four courgettes. Cut four gammon slices in 2.5cm/1in strips. Thread onto eight skewers, alternating courgettes and prunes. Grill for 4–5 minutes each side. Add juices to dressing and serve.

Pork and pepper stir fry

Serves 3–4 *Quick & Tasty*

Cut 450g/1lb pork fillet into strips. Toss in 1 tablespoon of cornflour. Fry in 2 tablespoons of oil for 2 minutes. Drain. Fry two crushed garlic cloves, one bunch of sliced spring onions, one small, sliced red and green pepper for 1 minute. Add 3 tablespoons of sherry, 1 tablespoon each demerara sugar and oil and seasoning. Add meat with one sliced mango and reheat.

Grilled lamb and goat's cheese

Serves 4 *Quick & Tasty*

Quarter 50g/2oz goat's cheese and press in chopped fresh rosemary. Fry four lamb noisettes or loin chops in 1 tablespoon of olive oil

Left: Skewered bacon

3 Baste very lean meat several times during roasting. Add parboiled potatoes and whole onions to the roasting tin for the final 1¼ hours of cooking, basting with meat juices or oil.

4 Transfer the cooked joint to a warmed serving plate. Cover the meat with foil and keep warm while you are making the Yorkshire puddings, cooking the prepared vegetables and making the gravy.

5 Drain off fat from pan, leaving the roasting juices. Add 300ml/½ pint prepared stock (see left, introduction), vegetable cooking liquid or wine. Season and bring to the boil, scraping up any residue in the pan.

for 7 minutes each side. Place a piece of cheese over each noisette and grill for 2 minutes until cheese has melted. Serve with pan-fried button mushrooms and cherry tomatoes.

Shredded veal with creamy vegetables

Serves 4

Thinly slice 450g/1lb veal escalope. Toss in 1 tablespoon of cornflour. Blend 300ml/½ pint double cream with 2 tablespoons each fresh chopped oregano and parsley, 1½ teaspoons of paprika and seasoning. Fry veal in 3 tablespoons of olive oil for 2 minutes. Drain. Fry 225g/8oz broccoli florets for 3 minutes. Add 225g/8oz sliced courgettes and 225g/8oz mangetout. Fry for 1 minute. Add meat. Heat cream and pour over.

Garlicky beef with ginger

Serves 2 *Quick & Tasty*

Shred 2.5cm/1in piece root ginger. Finely grate another 1cm/½in piece. Heat 1 tablespoon of sesame oil in a pan. Add 225g/8oz fillet steak in one piece. Fry gently, turning frequently, allowing 10 minutes for rare and 20 minutes for well done. Drain and keep warm. Gently fry grated ginger with two crushed garlic cloves for 1 minute. Add 1 teaspoon of soy sauce and 3 tablespoons of water. Heat through. Thinly slice steak and spoon over the sauce. Garnish with shredded ginger and chives. Serve with savoury fried rice.

Roasting chart

Sear all joints at 220C/425F/Gas 7, then reduce the temperature to 180C/350F/Gas 4 and roast as follows, allowing an extra 5 minutes per 450g/1lb for boned and rolled or stuffed joints of meat.

Beef
Rare	15 minutes per 450g/1lb + 15 minutes
Medium	20 minutes per 450g/1lb + 20 minutes
Well done	25 minutes per 450g/1lb + 25 minutes

Lamb
Medium	20 minutes per 450g/1lb + 20 minutes
Well done	30 minutes per 450g/1lb + 30 minutes

Pork
	35 minutes per 450g/1lb + 35 minutes

POT ROASTS

Pot roasting is suitable for tougher cuts, such as beef topside, silverside and brisket, and cheaper cuts of bacon or lean pork, which have a tendency to dry. Use a large pan or flameproof casserole with a tight-fitting lid. Simmer on the lowest setting or transfer to the oven and bake at 160C/325F/Gas 3 for 2–3 hours until tender. Remember, meat will shrink slightly during cooking. Once cooked, fattier joints can be cooled and the fat removed before reheating.

❶ Wipe and thoroughly dry meat on kitchen paper. Heat a little oil in a heavy-based, deep pan and fry it on all sides until it begins to colour, to seal in the juices. Drain off excess fat.

❷ Tuck plenty of vegetables, such as onions, carrots, celery, turnips or parsnips, around the meat. (Raising meat over vegetables will help to prevent the meat from burning during cooking.)

Bacon with watercress and beans

Serves 6

175g/6oz flageolets or haricot beans, soaked overnight in water
1.5kg/3lb unsmoked rolled gammon or bacon, soaked overnight in water

450g/1lb baby onions, peeled
3 carrots, thickly sliced
butter and flour, for thickening
50g/2oz watercress, roughly chopped
1 tbsp coarse-grain mustard
150ml/$\frac{1}{4}$ pint double cream

❶ Drain beans, bring to the boil in fresh water and boil rapidly for 10 minutes. Drain.
❷ Place meat in pan with onions and carrots (see step 2 above) and add 1.2 litres/2 pints of water. Bring to boil and cook as in step 4 above, for 2 hours, adding the beans after 1 hour.
❸ Drain meat, vegetables and beans. Thicken the juices with a blend of butter and flour, as in step 5 above right.
❹ Add watercress and mustard and half of the cream. Return meat and vegetables to pan, reheat and swirl with remaining cream.

❸ Add stock, water or a little wine, if desired, until the meat is two-thirds covered. Garlic, spices or herbs can also be added to give the meat extra flavour. Bring the liquid to the boil.

❹ Once it is boiling, skim off any scum that rises to the surface, using a slotted spoon. Reduce heat, cover with a tight fitting lid and simmer on the lowest heat for 2–3 hours until the meat is tender.

❺ To thicken the juices, remove the meat and vegetables to a warmed plate. Blend together 25g/1oz flour and 25g/1oz butter for each 1.2 litres/2 pints liquid, and whisk continuously until thickened.

Beef in a pot

Serves 6

1.5kg/3lb rolled silverside
1 celery stick, roughly chopped
1 onion, roughly chopped
2 bay leaves
12 juniper berries
150ml/$\frac{1}{4}$ pint red wine
150ml/$\frac{1}{4}$ pint red wine vinegar
1 tbsp oil
1 tbsp black treacle
12 pickled walnuts
seasoning
spring onions and carrots, to garnish

❶ Place meat in a deep dish. Surround with celery, onion, bay leaves and juniper. Pour over wine, vinegar and 300ml/$\frac{1}{2}$ pint water. Cover loosely, marinate in the fridge for 3 days, turning daily.

❷ Drain meat (reserving liquid and vegetables) and dry on kitchen paper. Fry in oil (see Pot roasts step 1 above left).

❸ Add the marinade vegetables and liquid and follow pot roasts steps 2, 3 and 4 as above, and simmer for 2 hours.

❹ Stir in treacle, walnuts and seasoning, heat through and add the garnishes.

From left: Bacon with watercress and beans and Beef in a pot

Casseroles

Look forward to those long evenings with these great ideas to pep up your winter menus. Try a hotpot of fish, chicken, lamb, pork, beef or rabbit, full of flavour and finished with a crunchy, unusual topping.

Beef and stout hotpot

Serves 6

3 tbsp oil

1kg/2lb braising steak, cubed

1 onion, thinly sliced

225g/8oz mushrooms, quartered

3 tbsp plain flour

300ml/$\frac{1}{2}$ pint Guinness

450ml/$\frac{3}{4}$ pint beef stock

2 tbsp tomato purée

2 tbsp Worcestershire sauce

2 tbsp pearl barley

seasoning

1kg/2lb potatoes, sliced

25g/1oz butter, melted

❶ Preheat the oven to 180C/350F/ Gas 4. Heat the oil in a flameproof casserole and brown beef. Lift, out.
❷ Fry onion for 5 minutes, add the mushrooms for 3 minutes. Replace beef, add flour and brown.
❸ Pour over the Guinness and stock. Add purée, Worcestershire sauce, barley and seasoning and bring to boil, stirring.
❹ Top with potatoes, season, and butter. Cover, bake for 1 hour. Remove lid; cook for 1 hour more.

Spiced pork with potato and parsnip scones

Serves 4

3 tbsp oil

675g/1$\frac{1}{2}$lb lean pork, diced

1 large onion, cut into wedges

2 carrots, diced

2 small parsnips, diced

$\frac{1}{2}$ tsp ground cumin

1 tsp ground turmeric

1 tsp coriander seeds, crushed

2 garlic cloves, crushed

2 tbsp plain flour

450ml/$\frac{3}{4}$ pint pork stock

seasoning

FOR THE SCONES

175g/6oz parsnips, diced

275g/10oz potatoes, diced

50g/2oz butter

100g/4oz self-raising flour

$\frac{1}{4}$ tsp ground turmeric

$\frac{1}{2}$ tsp coriander seeds, crushed

2 tsp oil, for frying

❶ Preheat the oven to 180C/ 350F/ Gas 4. Heat the oil in a flameproof casserole and brown pork. Lift out and set aside.

❷ Fry the diced vegetables for 5 minutes until lightly browned. Stir in spices, garlic and flour and cook for 1 minute. Pour on stock, add seasoning and pork and bring to boil.
❸ Cover and bake for 1$\frac{1}{4}$ hours or until pork is tender. Meanwhile, boil parsnips and potatoes in salted water until tender. Mash with butter.
❹ Stir in the flour and spices. Season to taste and mix to a smooth dough. Pat into an 18cm/7in round and cut into eight equal wedges. Brush a frying pan or griddle with oil and fry scones for 5 minutes on each side until golden. Serve hot with the pork casserole.

From left: Beef and stout hotpot, Spiced pork with potato and parsnip scones, Mediterranean lamb with herby croûtes, Mustard rabbit with sesame puffs and Chicken casserole with cheesy gougère (recipes page 88)

BASIC BEEF CASSEROLES

Casseroles are a great choice for a meal that will 'wait' if you want to eat later than expected – and they reheat well without spoiling. The cheaper the cut of meat, the longer the cooking time – between one and three hours allows the flavours to mingle.

Always fry the meat before the vegetables (otherwise it will steam rather than colour), and use a good, heavy-based pan.

❶ Wipe meat and trim off excess fat. For tender results, always cut the meat across the grain into small or large chunks, depending on personal preference.

❷ Season a little flour with salt and pepper and use it to coat the meat all over. Do this just before frying, so the flesh does not turn soggy.

Saffron spiced lamb

Serves 4

750g/1½lb lamb fillet or leg
1 tbsp plain flour
good pinch saffron threads
450ml/¾ pint chicken stock
3 tbsp olive oil
seasoning

1 onion, sliced
3 garlic cloves, crushed
1 small green chilli, chopped
2 bay leaves
2 cinnamon sticks
1 tbsp dark brown sugar
100g/4oz pre-soaked dried apricots
100g/4oz okra, trimmed

❶ Toss lamb in flour and fry in oil (see steps 1, 2 and 3 above). Transfer to an ovenproof dish.
❷ Soak saffron in 2 tablespoons boiling water for 30 minutes and add stock and seasoning. Fry onion, garlic, chilli, add bay leaves, cinnamon and sugar. Add to meat with apricots. Pour over stock. Cover and cook at 160C/325F/Gas 3 for 1¼ hours, adding okra for final 30 minutes.

3 Heat a little oil in a heavy-based frying pan or flameproof casserole. Add the meat a little at a time, and fry until it begins to brown on all sides.

4 Remove the meat with a slotted spoon. Add a little more oil if necessary and fry the vegetables until just softened. Combine with the meat in an ovenproof dish.

5 Bring the stock to the boil in a pan, scraping up any residue. Pour it over meat to cover. Cover tightly and cook in the centre of a slow oven.

Osso buco

Serves 6
6 thick slices shin of veal
2 tbsp olive oil
1 large onion, finely chopped
3 carrots, finely diced
3 celery sticks, finely diced
2 garlic cloves, crushed
400g/14oz can chopped tomatoes
grated rind and juice of 1 lemon
few fresh sprigs of thyme
150ml/$\frac{1}{4}$ pint chicken stock
150ml/$\frac{1}{4}$ pint dry white wine
seasoning

FOR THE GREMOLADA
3 tbsp chopped fresh parsley
grated rind of 1 lemon
2 garlic cloves, chopped

1 Tie veal with string. Preheat the oven to 180C/350F/Gas 4. Heat oil in a flameproof casserole and brown veal on both sides. Remove veal and set aside. Add the onion, carrots and celery. Fry until soft.

2 Stir in the remaining ingredients. Return veal to casserole, bring to the boil, cover and bake for 2 hours, turning veal once.

3 Mix gremolada ingredients together. Place veal on serving plates, sprinkle with the gremolada and serve.

From left: Saffron spiced lamb and Osso buco

Mediterranean lamb with herby croûtes

Serves 4

2 tbsp olive oil

4 lamb shoulder or chump chops, trimmed

2 carrots, halved lengthways and sliced diagonally

3 turnips, cut into wedges

2 garlic cloves, crushed

400g/14oz can chopped tomatoes

150ml/$\frac{1}{4}$ pint red wine

1 cinnamon stick, halved

2 bay leaves

seasoning

100g/4oz butter, softened

2 garlic cloves, crushed

3 tbsp chopped fresh mixed herbs

$\frac{1}{2}$ loaf French bread, sliced

❶ Preheat the oven to 180C/ 350F/Gas 4. Heat the oil in a flameproof casserole, add the lamb and brown all over. Lift out and set aside. Add the vegetables and garlic and fry for 5 minutes until soft.

❷ Return lamb to the casserole, add the tomatoes, wine, cinnamon, bay leaves and seasoning. Bring to boil, cover and bake for 1$\frac{1}{2}$ hours until lamb is tender.

❸ Beat the butter, garlic and herbs and toast the bread on one side. Turn bread over and spread with the herb butter. Just before serving, toast the buttered side of the bread. Arrange over lamb.

Mustard rabbit with sesame puffs

Serves 4

225g/8oz ready-made puff pastry

beaten egg, to glaze

2 tbsp sesame seeds

$\frac{1}{4}$ tsp paprika

25g/1oz plain flour

seasoning

4 rabbit joints

25g/1oz butter

1 tbsp oil

1 onion, finely chopped

1 apple, cored and sliced

300ml/$\frac{1}{2}$ pint chicken stock

1 tbsp coarse-grain mustard

150ml/$\frac{1}{4}$ pint soured cream

1 tsp cornflour

❶ Preheat the oven to 220C/ 425F/Gas 7. Roll out pastry on a floured surface and stamp out flower or heart shapes.

❷ Place the shapes on a greased baking sheet. Brush with egg, sprinkle with sesame seeds and paprika and bake for 8–10 minutes until risen and brown.

❸ Reduce oven to 180C/350F/ Gas 4. Mix flour and seasoning in a bag, add rabbit joints one at a time and toss.

❹ Heat butter and oil in a flameproof casserole. Shake off excess flour from rabbit, add joints to casserole and brown on both sides. Lift out and set aside. Add onion to casserole and fry for 5 minutes until softened, not browned.

❺ Stir in apple, stock, mustard and seasoning. Return rabbit and bring to boil. Cover and bake for 1 hour.

❻ Reheat pastry shapes at bottom of oven just before spooning rabbit on to serving plates. Mix cream and cornflour, stir into sauce, boil until thickened, spoon over rabbit.

Chicken casserole with cheesy gougère

Serves 4

2 tbsp olive oil

6 large boned, skinless chicken thighs, cubed

1 onion, sliced

2 tbsp plain flour

300ml/$\frac{1}{2}$ pint chicken stock

5 mini chorizo sausages, sliced

200g/7oz can sweetcorn, drained

seasoning

FOR THE GOUGÈRE

50g/2oz butter

60g/2$\frac{1}{2}$oz plain flour, sifted

2 eggs, beaten

100g/4oz Cheddar, grated

❶ Heat the oil in a flameproof casserole. Brown chicken, then lift out. Set aside.

❷ Soften onion in the casserole for 5 minutes, stir in flour and cook for 1 minute. Return chicken and add stock, sausage, sweetcorn and seasoning. Bring to the boil, stirring. Cover and simmer for 30 minutes.

❸ Heat 150ml/$\frac{1}{4}$ pint of water and the butter in a pan until water is boiling and butter has melted. Stir in the flour and remove pan from heat. Beat until mixture forms a smooth ball. Leave to cool.

❹ Preheat the oven to 220C/ 425F/Gas 7. Gradually beat the eggs into the flour mixture until smooth. Add half the cheese and season to taste.

❺ Spoon chicken into ovenproof dish draining off excess liquid (reserve and use for gravy). Spoon gougère around edge; sprinkle with remaining cheese. Shield chicken with foil. Bake for 30–35 minutes.

Thai-style chicken

Serves 4

2 chillies, roughly chopped, with seeds

1 small onion, chopped

2.5cm/1in root ginger, chopped

2 garlic cloves, halved

1 piece lemon grass, chopped

2 tsp paprika

$\frac{1}{2}$ tsp ground turmeric

$\frac{1}{4}$ tsp cumin seeds

$\frac{1}{4}$ tsp coriander seeds

1 tbsp anchovy essence

8 large skinless, boned chicken thighs, cut into pieces

400ml/14fl oz can coconut milk

chopped fresh coriander, to garnish

❶ Whizz ingredients (except the chicken, coconut milk and coriander) in a food processor. Spoon into a flameproof casserole, add chicken and coconut milk, bring to boil.

❷ Cover and simmer for 30 minutes, stirring occasionally, until the chicken is cooked. Sprinkle with coriander and serve with rice.

Beef olives

Serves 4

8 thin slices beef topside or sirloin

15g/$\frac{1}{2}$oz butter

1 tbsp olive oil

1 small onion, finely chopped

1 red pepper, seeded and chopped

1 carrot, diced

1 garlic clove, crushed

1 tbsp plain flour

150ml/$\frac{1}{4}$ pint beef stock

FOR THE STUFFING

75g/3oz ricotta

175g/6oz mushrooms, chopped

6 sun-dried tomatoes, chopped

2 tsp red pesto

seasoning

100g/4oz garlic sausage, thinly sliced

❶ Beat out each beef slice between greaseproof paper until they are half as big again. Preheat the oven to 180C/350F/Gas 4.

❷ For the stuffing, mix the ricotta, mushrooms, tomatoes, red pesto and seasoning.

❸ Divide garlic sausage among the beef. Spoon stuffing on each slice, roll up, tucking in ends. Tie with string.

❹ Heat the butter and oil in a shallow, flameproof casserole. Add the beef and brown all over. Lift out; set aside.

❺ Add vegetables and fry until soft. Add garlic and flour; cook for 1 minute. Stir in the stock, seasoning and beef. Bring to the boil, cover and bake for 45 minutes. Lift out beef, remove string and keep hot. Purée sauce. Serve with tagliatelle.

Below: Beef olives

Fish Creole

Serves 4

2 tbsp olive oil

1 onion, finely chopped

1 garlic clove, crushed

400g/14oz can chopped tomatoes

grated rind and juice of 1 lemon

seasoning

750g/1½lb cod fillet, in 4 pieces

275g/10oz mixed fresh fish and shellfish

300g/11oz jar artichoke hearts, drained

flat leaf parsley, to garnish

❶ Heat the oil in a shallow, flameproof casserole and fry the onion for about 5 minutes until softened.

❷ Stir in the garlic, tomatoes, lemon rind and juice. Season, add the cod, then scatter fish, shellfish and artichokes on top. Cover and simmer for 10–12 minutes until the cod can be flaked with a knife.

❸ Spoon on to serving plates, garnish with parsley and serve with brown rice. If you prefer, you can use another chunky white fish, such as haddock, pollack, ling or monkfish – or smoked cod or smoked haddock.

Pork and peppers

Serves 4

2 tbsp olive oil

1 green, 1 red, 1 yellow, 1 orange pepper, seeded and thickly sliced

4 boneless loin pork chops

2 garlic cloves, crushed

2 tbsp tomato purée

150ml/¼ pint pork stock

seasoning

❶ Heat olive oil in a flameproof casserole. Add the peppers and fry over a high heat for 5 minutes,

stirring all the time until the peppers are browned. Lift them out of the casserole with a slotted spoon and set aside in a bowl.

❷ Trim the pork, add to the casserole and fry for 5 minutes on each side until browned. Add the garlic, tomato purée, pork stock and seasoning. Return the peppers to the casserole, cover and simmer for 10 minutes until the chops are cooked. Spoon on to serving plates and serve with boiled new potatoes.

Turkey, Ricard and yogurt sauté

Serves 4

25g/1oz butter

1 tbsp oil

8 turkey breast slices

1 fennel bulb, halved and sliced

grated rind and juice of ½ orange

6 tbsp Ricard

seasoning

4 tbsp Greek strained yogurt

1 tsp cornflour

2 tsp chopped fresh fennel

❶ Heat the butter and oil together in a shallow, flameproof casserole. Add the turkey and brown it on both sides. Add the sliced fennel and continue to cook for about 3–4 minutes until it is just beginning to soften. Stir in the orange rind, orange juice and the Ricard. Season the mixture, cover the casserole and simmer for 10 minutes.

❷ Mix the Greek yogurt and cornflour together. Pour into the casserole and sprinkle with the chopped fennel. Cook for 1 minute, stirring continuously.

Speedy Irish stew

Serves 4

25g/1oz butter

1 tbsp oil

450g/1lb lamb fillet, sliced

1 parsnip, diced

2 carrots, diced

1 large turnip, diced

½ small swede, diced

2 potatoes, diced

1 onion, finely sliced

2 tbsp plain flour

600ml/1 pint lamb stock

2 fresh sprigs of rosemary

seasoning

2 leeks, sliced

FOR THE DUMPLINGS

225g/8oz self-raising flour

pinch of salt

100g/4oz shredded suet

3 tbsp chopped fresh parsley

1 tsp chopped fresh rosemary

❶ Heat the butter and oil in a flameproof casserole. Add the lamb a few pieces at a time and fry until evenly brown. Remove lamb with a slotted spoon. Add the root vegetables and onion, fry for 5 minutes, stirring until softened.
❷ Stir in flour and cook for 1 minute. Add the stock, rosemary sprigs and seasoning. Return lamb to casserole and bring to the boil. Cover and simmer for 15 minutes, stirring occasionally.
❸ Meanwhile, make the dumplings. Mix together the flour, salt, suet and herbs. Add 9–10 tablespoons of water and mix to a soft, not sticky dough. Shape into balls with floured hands.
❹ Add the leeks, then the dumplings to the simmering stew. Cover and simmer for 15 minutes until the leeks are tender and the dumplings well risen.

Devilled kidneys

Serves 4

6 lambs' kidneys

2 tbsp oil

225g/8oz cocktail sausages

25g/1oz butter

2 rashers streaky bacon, chopped

175g/6oz pickling onions or shallots, halved

2 tbsp plain flour

150ml/$\frac{1}{4}$ pint lamb stock

1 tbsp tomato purée

2 tsp coarse-grain mustard

1 tbsp Worcestershire sauce

seasoning

❶ Halve the kidneys with a sharp knife, then cut away the white central core with kitchen scissors.
❷ Heat the oil in a shallow, flameproof casserole, add the cocktail sausages and fry for

5 minutes, stirring occasionally, until they are all evenly browned. Lift the sausages out of the casserole and set aside.
❸ Add the butter to the casserole and when it has melted, add the bacon, onions and kidneys and cook, stirring, for 5 minutes until everything is browned.
❹ Stir in the flour and cook for 1 minute then stir in the stock, the browned sausages and remaining ingredients. Simmer for 3–4 minutes until the kidneys are cooked.

From left: Pork and peppers, Turkey, Ricard and yoghurt sauté, Speedy Irish stew and Devilled kidneys

Pulses

Protein-rich pulses can be used as the basis of many delicious hot meals, snacks and salads. Get the best from your beans, peas and lentils with these easy-to-use, tasty recipes.

Trio of stuffed vegetables

Serves 4

1 onion, chopped

2 garlic cloves, crushed

3 tbsp olive oil

175g/6oz yellow split peas, soaked

$\frac{1}{2}$ tsp dried thyme

2 tbsp chopped fresh chives

300ml/$\frac{1}{2}$ pint chicken or vegetable stock

seasoning

1 small aubergine

2 courgettes

2 beefsteak tomatoes

100g/4oz mozzarella, grated

❶ Fry onion and garlic in 2 tablespoons of the olive oil.

❷ Add drained peas, herbs and stock and bring to the boil. Reduce heat and simmer gently until liquid is absorbed and peas are tender, about 25 minutes. Season well.

❸ Simmer aubergine in boiling water for 8 minutes. Halve aubergine and courgettes lengthways. Scoop out centres, leaving a 5mm/$\frac{1}{4}$in shell, and chop the flesh. Remove a slice from the tops of the tomatoes and scoop out seeds. Brush inside aubergine and courgettes with remaining oil.

❹ Add the cheese and chopped courgette and aubergine to the peas and pack into the vegetable cases. Bake at 180C/350F/Gas 4 for 30 minutes.

From left: Trio of stuffed vegetables and Curried chickpeas with chutney (recipe page 94)

PEAS AND CHICKPEAS

Both peas and chickpeas need thorough soaking to soften them before cooking, and cooking times will vary. All dried peas have a shelf life of up to a year – any longer and they may well need extra cooking, or possibly not soften at all.

Pea and ham soup

Bought whole or skinned and split, dried peas are classically combined with smoked ham or bacon in a richly flavoured soup.

❶ Cover 450g/1lb whole dried peas with cold water and leave to soak overnight in a cool place. Drain peas, place in a large pan. Cover with plenty of clean water.

❷ Bring the peas to the boil and cook rapidly for 10 minutes, skimming off any scum that rises to the surface of the water with a spoon. Drain the peas in a colander and set them aside.

❸ Chop and fry two carrots, one onion, two celery sticks, two bay leaves and a sprig of thyme in 3 tablespoons of oil until softened. Add a 450–900g/1–2lb bacon knuckle and the drained peas to the pan of vegetables.

❹ Just cover with cold water and bring to the boil. Reduce heat and simmer for 2–3 hours until the meat is tender. Remove the meat and transfer it to a chopping board.

❺ Cut meat into chunks, discarding skin and bones. Return to pan with seasoning and a little chopped mint, if you like. Serve as a chunky soup, blend coarsely, or process to a smooth purée.

Curried chickpeas

Serves 4–6

| 350g/12oz chickpeas, soaked |
| 2 large onions, chopped |
| 3 garlic cloves, crushed |
| 1 red or green chilli, chopped |
| 4cm/1½in piece fresh root ginger, peeled and grated |
| 1 tsp ground coriander |
| 1 tsp cumin seeds |
| ½ tsp ground turmeric |
| 5 tbsp oil |
| 400g/14oz can chopped tomatoes |
| 2 tsp muscovado sugar |
| 1 tbsp garam masala |
| seasoning |

❶ Boil chickpeas for about 30 minutes until they are just tender, then drain.

❷ Fry the onions, garlic, chilli, ginger, coriander, cumin and turmeric in the oil.

❸ Add the chickpeas, tomatoes, sugar, garam masala and seasoning to taste, and cook for 30 minutes over a very gentle heat, stirring frequently. Serve hot as a main course; also tasty cold with a flavoursome chutney.

Right: Their variety in shape and colour make pulses an eye-catching display for your kitchen shelves

Chilli beans

Serves 2–3

Fry one chopped onion and one chopped celery stick in 3 tablespoons of oil. Add $\frac{1}{2}$ teaspoon of chilli powder, $\frac{1}{2}$ teaspoon of ground coriander, a 225g/8oz can of chopped tomatoes, $\frac{1}{2}$ teaspoon of sugar and a drained and rinsed 400g/14oz can of red kidney beans. Simmer gently for 20 minutes. Serve with slices of avocado and soured cream.

Below: Lemony bean Stroganoff with baked potato

Spicy sausages with black beans

Serves 4

Put 450g/1lb spicy sausages in a large frying pan with 2 tablespoons of oil, two garlic cloves, two bay leaves and one cinnamon stick. Fry gently for 10 minutes. Add a drained 400g/14oz can of black-eyed beans, 150ml/$\frac{1}{4}$ pint water and $\frac{1}{4}$ teaspoon of nutmeg. Season and cook for 15 minutes until the sausages are cooked through.

Sprouting bean salad

Serves 4

Lightly fry 225g/8oz baby sweetcorn and one bunch of chopped spring onions in 5 tablespoons of sesame oil. Add 100g/4oz oyster or button mushrooms and 100g/4oz trimmed mangetout to the frying pan, then cook for 2 minutes, stirring constantly. Add 225g/8oz mixed sprouting beans and 2 tablespoons of soy sauce. Heat through gently, mixing thoroughly with the other ingredients.

To pressure cook peas and beans

Weigh the dried beans or peas, soak them overnight in cold water, then drain. Use 1.2 litres/2 pints water for every 450g/1lb dry weight of the beans or peas. (It is important that the cooker should not be more than half filled.)

❶ Place the required amount of water and the beans or peas in the pressure cooker. Bring to the boil, then skim the surface to remove any foam. Reduce the heat, cover and bring to high pressure.

❷ Allow about one third of the usual cooking time. Normally, most beans take about 45 minutes to cook, so allow 15 minutes in the pressure cooker. Peas will take a few minutes longer than beans to soften. There is no need to rapid boil peas or beans beforehand when using a pressure cooker as the high temperature removes the toxins.

Pulse and pasta ragoût

Serves 4 *Quick & Tasty*

Lightly fry one bunch of chopped spring onions, and two garlic cloves in 40g/1¼oz butter and 1 tablespoon of oil. Add 100g/ 4oz brown rice, 100g/4oz whole lentils and 300ml/½ pint stock. Cover and simmer until tender, adding more water if necessary. Stir in three chopped tomatoes, 100g/4oz cooked pasta shapes and 2 tablespoons of chopped fresh mint. Season well and heat through gently before serving.

Lemony bean Stroganoff

Serves 4 *Quick & Tasty*

Fry one sliced onion in 2 tablespoons of oil. Add 100g/ 4oz sliced mushrooms, the grated rind of one lemon, 1 teaspoon of sugar, 2 teaspoons of coarse mustard, ¼ teaspoon of freshly chopped mixed herbs and 85ml/ 3fl oz double cream. Add a drained and rinsed 400g/14oz can of red kidney beans and a drained and rinsed 225g/8oz can of flageolet or haricot beans. Season and heat through, adding water if too thick.

Below: Sprouting bean salad

LENTILS

Whole brown and green lentils are quicker to cook than other pulses and do not need pre-soaking. Split red lentils cook even more quickly and soon turn to 'mush' – beware. Rinse lentils before use and check for stones and husks.

Chicken and lentils

Lentils need plenty of fresh spices, herbs and seasoning.

❶ To cook with lentils for salads, fill a pan with water and add chunks of onion and a bay leaf. Bring to the boil and simmer for 10–25 minutes until lentils are just tender.

❷ For casseroles, cook the lentils, as follows. Fry one sliced onion, $\frac{1}{2}$ teaspoon of turmeric, two cinnamon sticks, 12 cardamom pods and one dried chilli in oil.

Mixed lentil salad with watercress mayonnaise

Serves 6

150g/5oz natural yogurt

4 tbsp mayonnaise

$\frac{1}{2}$ bunch watercress, finely chopped

100g/4oz each of brown, green and split red lentils, cooked and drained (see step 2, above)

1 bunch spring onions, chopped

1 small orange pepper and 1 red pepper, finely chopped

grated rind of 1 lemon

6 tbsp olive oil

2 tbsp chopped fresh parsley

frilly lettuce leaves

12 quail's eggs, hard-boiled

seasoning

❶ Beat together the natural yogurt, mayonnaise, watercress and seasoning. Spoon into a serving bowl.

❷ Mix together the brown, green and red lentils, spring onions, both peppers, lemon rind, oil, parsley and seasoning.

❸ Line serving dishes with the lettuce leaves and spoon the salad into centre. Garnish with halved quail's eggs and serve as a starter or as a main course with the watercress-flavoured mayonnaise.

3 Add 6–8 chicken pieces and fry for 5 minutes on all sides. Weigh and rinse 175g/6oz split red lentils and add to the casserole, spooning around the meat.

4 Pour water into casserole until the chicken portions are just covered. Add a tight-fitting lid or foil and cook at 180C/350F/Gas 4 for 1 hour.

5 Once cooked, the lentils should have absorbed all of the water and feel soft in texture. Season them with salt and pepper, then serve hot.

Garlicky mixed lentils

Serves 6

2 onions, chopped

2 garlic cloves, crushed

3 tbsp olive oil

3 bay leaves

$\frac{1}{2}$ tsp dried thyme

900ml/1$\frac{1}{2}$ pints chicken stock

225g/8oz green or brown lentils

225g/8oz split red lentils

3 tomatoes, finely diced

2 tbsp chopped fresh parsley

$\frac{1}{2}$ tsp salt

1 Fry onions and garlic in oil until soft.

2 Add the bay leaves, thyme, stock and green or brown lentils. Bring to the boil, then reduce the heat, cover and simmer gently for 15 minutes.

3 Add red lentils and cook for a further 10 minutes until they are tender, but still retain their shape. Stir in the diced tomatoes, parsley and salt. Serve the lentils hot on warmed plates with crusty bread.

From left: Mixed lentil salad with watercress mayonnaise and Garlicky mixed lentils

BEANS

Dried beans include black, red, white, butter, black-eyed, borlotti, flageolet, soya, mung, haricot and aduki. Sprouting beans enliven salads.

Pork and beans

Most beans need soaking (preferably overnight) before use, and all beans must be boiled rapidly for 10 minutes to destroy toxins. Always cook thoroughly.

❶ To make baked beans, bring 350g/12oz haricot beans to the boil in unsalted water. Boil for 10 minutes, skimming off any scum. Then simmer for 1 hour until tender.

❷ In a large flameproof casserole, fry one large chopped onion and 100g/4oz salt pork or streaky bacon for 5 minutes until they have turned golden brown.

Beans with pasta and pistou

Serves 4

100g/4oz each black-eyed, butter and aduki beans

large bunch of fresh basil

3 garlic cloves

1 tomato, diced, plus 100g/4oz tomatoes, halved

50g/2oz Parmesan

100ml/4fl oz olive oil

25g/1oz butter

4 courgettes, sliced

1 onion, sliced

100g/4oz mushrooms, halved if large

175g/6oz tagliatelle verde

black olives and basil leaves, to garnish

❶ Soak beans overnight, rinse and cover with plenty of cold water. Boil rapidly for 10 minutes, and simmer according to directions until tender. Drain, rinse and set aside.

❷ To make the pistou, blend the basil, garlic, diced tomato and Parmesan in a food processor or blender. Gradually add the oil, blending to a thick paste.

❸ Melt the butter in a pan. Add the courgettes and onion and fry gently for 4 minutes. Stir in mushrooms and tomatoes.

❹ Cook pasta in plenty of boiling, salted water until just tender. Drain and add to the pan with the beans. Heat through gently while tossing all the ingredients together. Be careful not to break up or mash the beans. Remove from heat.

❺ Divide among four hot plates, garnish with olives and basil and serve with pistou, which can be tossed into the salad or served separately.

❸ Drain the beans, reserving 600ml/1 pint of the cooking juices. Add the beans to the onion and pork or bacon in the casserole and stir thoroughly.

❹ Blend a little cooking juice with 2 tablespoons each black treacle and tomato purée and 1 tablespoon of coarse-grain mustard. Stir in remaining liquid.

❺ Pour the liquid over the beans and cover the dish with a tight-fitting lid. Bake at 150C/300F/Gas 2 for 2–3 hours until beans are completely tender. Serve hot.

Cassoulet

Serves 4–6

225g/8oz smoked streaky bacon, cubed

450g/1lb pork, cubed

2 duck breasts

4 tbsp oil

2 onions, sliced

6 garlic cloves, crushed

1 celery stick, chopped

3 bay leaves

1 tbsp chopped fresh oregano

450g/1lb mixed beans, boiled and drained

100g/4oz breadcrumbs

seasoning

❶ Fry bacon, pork and duck in oil and transfer to a large casserole. Gently fry onions, garlic and celery in a frying pan.

❷ Add bay leaves and 300ml/½ pint water to pan and bring to boil. Add oregano, beans and vegetables to casserole, pour pan juices over beans and water to almost cover. Sprinkle with half the breadcrumbs and season.

❸ Cover and bake at 150C/300F/Gas 2 for 2 hours. Push breadcrumbs into dish to thicken juices, sprinkle with remainder and bake for 1 hour.

From left: Beans with pasta and pistou and Cassoulet

Vegetables

Available now in such abundance, get the
most from your vegetables with these
appetizing, colourful and original recipes that
can be served as an accompaniment main meal.

Left: Vegetables with bruschetta

Vegetables with bruschetta

Serves 6 as a starter

6 small tomatoes

12 open cap mushrooms

1 yellow and 1 green pepper, seeded and cut into eight pieces

4 garlic cloves, crushed

1 tsp golden caster sugar

2 tbsp chopped fresh parsley

2 tsp chopped fresh thyme

4 tbsp red wine

5 tbsp olive oil

seasoning

6 slices of French bread

❶ Preheat the oven to 190C/ 375F/Gas 5. Cut a small cross in the top of each tomato and trim mushroom stalks. Arrange tomatoes, mushrooms and peppers in an ovenproof dish.
❷ Mix half of the garlic with the sugar, parsley, thyme, wine and 3 tablespoons of the olive oil. Pour over the vegetables and season. Bake for 15–20 minutes.
❸ Meanwhile, place the French bread slices on an oiled wire rack and toast until brown. Mix together the remaining garlic and olive oil, drizzle over the toast and sprinkle with black pepper. Serve hot with the vegetables.

Roast potatoes with a salt crust

Serves 4

500g/1lb new or small old potatoes, scrubbed

4 tbsp oil

1 tbsp salt flakes

❶ Cook potatoes in boiling water for 5 minutes. Drain and cool. Slash with a knife and put into a roasting tin with the oil.

❷ Cook on a high shelf until browned. Turn and baste with oil several times during cooking.
❸ Sprinkle salt over the potatoes 5 minutes before the end of cooking. Serve potatoes hot.

Courgettes with mozzarella

Serves 4

250g/8oz each green and yellow courgettes, sliced diagonally

1 tbsp olive oil

1 tbsp vegetable oil

1 garlic clove, chopped

1 tsp white wine vinegar

2 tsp fresh chopped basil

seasoning

50g/2oz mozzarella cheese, grated

❶ Plunge courgettes into a pan of boiling water and cook for 30 seconds. Drain, rinse with cold water and drain again. Arrange alternate colours in a shallow dish.
❷ Mix the oils, garlic, vinegar, basil and seasoning together and drizzle over courgettes. Sprinkle with cheese. Grill for 5–10 minutes until hot.

Trio of glazed vegetables

Serves 4

250g/½lb turnips, cut into wedges

250g/½lb carrots, sliced

4 sticks of celery, sliced

25g/1oz butter

1 tbsp soft light brown sugar

juice of ½ orange

25g/1oz walnut pieces

seasoning

celery leaves, to garnish

❶ Cook the turnips and carrots in a pan of boiling, salted water until just tender. Add celery, cook for 1 minute, then drain.

❷ Melt butter in the pan, add the sugar and orange juice and heat gently until the sugar has dissolved, then bring to the boil.
❸ Return the vegetables to the pan, add the walnuts and seasoning. Cook for 3–4 minutes, stirring until browned. Spoon into a warmed serving dish and garnish with celery leaves. Serve hot.

Baked aubergines

Serves 4

450g/1lb baby aubergines, halved

salt

4 tbsp fresh breadcrumbs

4 tbsp grated Parmesan

50g/2oz pitted black olives, chopped

4 tbsp olive oil

6 tbsp chopped fresh parsley

25g/1oz capers, rinsed and chopped

❶ Place aubergines in a colander and sprinkle with salt. Set aside to drain for 30 minutes.
❷ Preheat the oven to 200C/ 400F/Gas 6. Mix together the breadcrumbs, cheese and olives. Heat half the oil in a frying pan and fry this mixture until it turns golden brown.
❸ Rinse the aubergines thoroughly and cook in boiling, salted water for 3 minutes. Drain and arrange aubergines, cut side up, in an oiled baking dish.
❹ Mix the parsley and capers into the breadcrumb mixture and sprinkle over the aubergines. Drizzle over the remaining oil.
❺ Bake for 20 minutes until tender. Serve hot or cold.

Braised fennel with spiced couscous

Serves 4

2 large heads of fennel, trimmed

3 tbsp olive oil

1 garlic clove, chopped

675g/1½lb ripe tomatoes

150ml/¼ pint white wine

4 sprigs of thyme

1 bay leaf

pinch of sugar

225g/8oz couscous

50g/2oz butter, softened

1 tsp paprika

½ tsp cayenne pepper

1 tbsp chopped fresh coriander

seasoning

fresh thyme, to garnish

❶ Quarter the fennel heads lengthways. Heat the oil in a large pan and fry the fennel and garlic for about 10 minutes until the fennel is browned on all sides. Remove with a slotted spoon and set aside.

❷ Peel and seed the tomatoes over a bowl to catch the juices, add the flesh and juice to the pan with the wine and boil rapidly for 5 minutes. Add the thyme, bay leaf and sugar and place the fennel in the pan in a single layer. Cover and simmer for about 20 minutes or until the fennel is just tender.

❸ Meanwhile, wash the couscous under running water and leave to moisten for about 10 minutes. Fluff the grains with a fork and place in a steamer. Steam the couscous for 10–12 minutes until all the grains are puffed up and tender.

❹ While the couscous and fennel are cooking, cream together the butter, paprika, cayenne pepper, coriander and seasoning. When the couscous is ready, transfer to a bowl and stir in the spiced butter mixture until evenly coated. Serve the braised fennel at once on a bed of couscous garnished with the thyme.

Below: Braised fennel with spiced couscous

Vegetable platter with herb aïoli

Serves 4

FOR THE AÏOLI

2 egg yolks

1 garlic clove, crushed

$\frac{1}{2}$ tsp salt

$\frac{1}{2}$ tsp cayenne pepper

1 tsp lemon juice

250ml/8fl oz light olive oil

25g/1oz fresh herbs, such as chervil, chives and mint, finely chopped

FOR THE PLATTER

100g/4oz purple sprouting broccoli, trimmed

100g/4oz baby carrots, trimmed

100g/4oz frozen broad beans

1 bunch radishes, trimmed

25g/1oz rocket

25g/1oz salad leaves

4 canned artichoke hearts, drained and quartered

❶ Make the aïoli: whisk the egg yolks, garlic, salt, cayenne pepper and lemon juice until pale and creamy. Gradually whisk in the olive oil until the mixture is a thick mayonnaise consistency – add a little hot water if too thick. Stir in the herbs, then pour into a small dish, cover and set aside.

❷ Steam the broccoli and carrots for 2–3 minutes, then add the broad beans and steam for 1 minute until just tender. Plunge into cold water, drain and pat dry with kitchen paper.

❸ Spoon the aïoli into the centre of a plate and surround with all of the vegetables rocket, salad leaves and artichokes. Serve with Cheese and herb bun loaf (see page 129).

Spring vegetable risotto with goat's cheese

Serves 4

50g/2oz butter

1 onion, chopped

1 garlic clove, crushed

275g/10oz arborio (risotto) rice

150ml/$\frac{1}{4}$ pint dry white wine

750ml/1$\frac{1}{4}$ pints vegetable stock

225g/8oz spring greens, shredded

100g/4oz frozen broad beans

25g/1oz rocket or watercress

1 tbsp lemon juice

2 tbsp chopped fresh herbs, such as mint and chervil

100g/4oz goat's cheese, crumbled

seasoning

Parmesan shavings, to garnish

lemon wedges, to serve

❶ Melt the butter in a large pan and gently fry the onion and garlic for 10 minutes. Add the arborio rice, stir fry for 1 minute, then pour in the wine and simmer, stirring continuously, until the excess liquid evaporates.

❷ Reserve 150ml/$\frac{1}{4}$ pint of the stock. Add the rest of the stock, a ladleful at a time, and cook for about 20 minutes until the liquid is absorbed and the rice is tender.

❸ Blanch the spring greens in boiling, salted water for 2–3 minutes, then drain.

❹ Stir the remaining stock into the rice along with the spring greens and broad beans and cook, stirring, for 3 minutes. Add the rocket or watercress, lemon juice, chopped herbs, goat's cheese and seasoning to taste. Pile the risotto on to a large serving plate and garnish with the Parmesan shavings. Serve immediately with wedges of lemon.

Leek, goat's cheese and olive flan

Serves 8

6 large leeks, trimmed

300ml/$\frac{1}{2}$ pint vegetable stock

450g/1 lb ready-made puff pastry

2 tbsp olive paste

175g/6oz goat's cheese, thinly sliced

flour, to dust

1 egg

1 tbsp milk

pinch of salt

2 tbsp sesame seeds

new potatoes, courgettes and French beans, to serve

❶ Preheat oven to 200C/400F/ Gas 6. Wash leeks and poach in the stock for 3–4 minutes until tender. Drain.

❷ Roll out half the pastry to a rectangle 20 × 25cm/8 × 10in and transfer to a large baking sheet. Spread over olive paste, leaving a 1cm/$\frac{1}{2}$in border around the edge.

❸ Arrange the leeks lengthways over the paste and top with the cheese. Brush edges with water.

❹ Roll out the remaining pastry to a slightly larger rectangle, 23 × 28cm/9 × 11in. Dust lightly with flour, fold in half lengthways and, using a sharp knife, cut crossways through the folded edge at 1cm/$\frac{1}{2}$in intervals. Open out the pastry and use to top leeks, pressing edges together to seal. Knock up and flute the edges.

❺ Combine the egg, milk and salt, brush over the pastry and sprinkle with sesame seeds. Bake for 25–30 minutes until golden. Serve with accompaniments.

Root vegetable couscous with two sauces

Serves 4

3 tbsp olive oil
4 baby onions, halved
2 garlic cloves, crushed
1 dried red chilli, crushed
1 tsp each ground cinnamon, cumin, coriander and turmeric
225g/8oz carrots, sliced
175g/6oz each celeriac, swede and sweet potato, cubed
300ml/$\frac{1}{2}$ pint tomato juice
150ml/$\frac{1}{4}$ pint vegetable stock
100g/4oz cooked chickpeas
75g/3oz raisins
2 tbsp chopped parsley
350g/12oz couscous
knob of butter
$\frac{1}{2}$ tsp hot chilli sauce
1 tbsp lemon juice
1 tbsp chopped fresh parsley
40g/1$\frac{1}{2}$oz cashew nuts, toasted, to garnish

FOR THE GREEN SAUCE
2 tbsp chopped fresh coriander
1 garlic clove, chopped
1 tbsp chopped toasted cashew nuts
grated rind of 1 lime, plus 1 tsp lime juice
3 tbsp olive oil
seasoning

❶ Heat oil; fry onions, garlic, chilli and spices for 2 minutes. Add vegetables, stir fry for 5 minutes. Add juice and stock, bring to boil. Cover; simmer for 15 minutes. Add chickpeas, raisins and parsley and simmer for 15 minutes.
❷ Blend the green sauce ingredients except oil in food processor. Stir in oil and season.
❸ Wash couscous in a sieve and leave for 10 minutes. Fluff up grains, then steam for 10 minutes until soft. Toss with butter, place in serving dish.
❹ Strain juices from stew, stir remaining ingredients into juices to make a red sauce.

❺ Pile vegetables on top of couscous, sprinkle over nuts and serve with both sauces.

Parsnip and mustard tatin

Serves 8–10

150g/5oz plain flour
pinch of salt
1 tsp chopped fresh sage
90g/3$\frac{1}{2}$oz butter, diced
25g/1oz walnuts, toasted and ground
1 egg yolk
FOR THE TOPPING
75g/3oz unsalted butter
675g/1$\frac{1}{2}$lb small parsnips
25g/1oz walnuts, chopped
300ml/$\frac{1}{2}$ pint vegetable stock
2 tbsp wholegrain mustard
2 tbsp clear honey
tagliatelle and mangetout, to serve

❶ Sift flour and salt into a bowl. Stir in sage. Rub in butter until it resembles fine breadcrumbs. Stir in walnuts. Add egg yolk and 2–3 tablespoons of water to form a soft dough. Wrap and chill for 30 minutes.
❷ Preheat oven to 200C/400F/ Gas 6. Melt the butter in a 20cm/ 8in ovenproof frying pan. Halve the parsnips. Arrange, cut side up, to fit snugly in pan. Fry for 6–8 minutes until well browned underneath. Sprinkle over the walnuts.
❸ Boil the stock, mustard and honey together until reduced by half and pour over parsnips.
❹ Roll out pastry a little larger than pan. Cover parsnips, pressing pastry down sides. Bake for 20–25 minutes until crisp. Leave for 5 minutes. Turn out on to a plate to catch juices. Serve with vegetables.

Left: Parsnip and mustard tatin

Courgette and tomato tart

Serves 4

2 tbsp olive oil

2 onions, sliced

1 tbsp caster sugar

3 large tomatoes, thinly sliced

1 courgette, thinly sliced

seasoning

2 tsp chopped fresh oregano or
1 tsp dried

175g/6oz ready-made shortcrust
pastry

fresh oregano leaves, to garnish
(optional)

❶ Preheat the oven to 200C/ 400F/Gas 6. Heat the oil in a heavy-based pan and fry the onions for about 5 minutes until flecked with brown. Sprinkle with sugar and stir for 1 minute, then add 3 tablespoons of water and simmer until tender.

❷ Spoon the onion mixture into a shallow 20cm/8in round sandwich tin. Arrange the tomatoes and courgette in an overlapping layer. Season and sprinkle over the oregano.

❸ Roll out the pastry to a 25cm/ 10in round and place over the vegetables, tucking the edges down the side of the tin. Trim, place on a baking sheet and bake for 20–25 minutes or until the pastry is deep brown. Turn out on to a serving dish, scatter over the oregano leaves, if using, and serve hot or warm.

Below: Courgette and tomato tart

Batters

Simple batters can be used as the basis for a surprisingly wide variety of dishes, both savoury and sweet. Follow the step-by-step instructions for really perfect pancakes, puddings and fritters.

Apricot and Amaretto pancakes

Serves 4

4 sugar lumps, crushed

1 orange

25g/1oz unsalted butter

50g/2oz caster sugar

175g/6oz no-need-to-soak dried apricots

300ml/$\frac{1}{2}$ pint apricot or tropical fruit juice

50g/2oz Amaretti or macaroon biscuits

8 prepared pancakes (see overleaf)

3 tbsp Amaretto liqueur

extra biscuits and crushed sugar lumps, to decorate

whipped cream, to serve

❶ Rub the sugar lumps over the orange to remove the zest, then crush the lumps.

❷ Melt the butter in a frying pan. Add the crushed sugar and caster sugar, dried apricots and fruit juice. Simmer gently for about 10 minutes. Place the biscuits in a bowl and crush gently. Drain the apricots and reserve the juice.

❸ Coat the pancakes in the juice on both sides. Sprinkle each one with crushed biscuits and fold into quarters.

❹ Return the folded pancakes to the pan with the apricots and liqueur and heat through gently. Watch the pancakes carefully as you do not want the liquid to boil dry.

❺ Sprinkle the pancakes with the extra biscuits and sugar lumps to decorate. Serve topped with whipped cream.

From left: Apricot and Amaretto pancakes and Savoury pancake layer (recipe overleaf)

PANCAKES

Pancake batter can be savoury or sweet. Wholemeal or buckwheat flour can be substituted for half the plain flour, add an extra 3 tablespoons milk to thin the buckwheat batter. Cooked pancakes can be frozen between greaseproof paper but don't keep them for longer than one month.

Makes 8–10 pancakes

100g/4 oz plain flour

pinch of salt

1 egg

300ml/$\frac{1}{2}$ pint milk

❶ Sift the flour and salt into a bowl. Make a well in the centre. Break the egg into the well and add a little milk. Whisk egg and milk, gradually incorporating the flour to make a smooth batter. Beat in remaining milk.

❷ Heat a little oil in a medium frying pan. Drain off excess. Pour in a little batter, tilting the pan as you pour until the batter thinly coats the base. Cook over a moderate heat until golden on the underside.

Savoury pancake layer

Serves 6

225g/8oz mozzarella cheese

100g/4oz walnuts, chopped

1 tbsp chopped fresh oregano

2 garlic cloves, crushed

seasoning

450g/1lb tomatoes

3 small courgettes

2 tbsp olive oil

8 prepared buckwheat pancakes (see introduction, and steps above)

Parmesan cheese, to serve

❶ Finely dice half of the mozzarella; slice remainder. Mix diced cheese with the walnuts, oregano, garlic and seasoning.
❷ Slice the tomatoes and courgettes. Heat the oil in a frying pan. Add the courgettes and fry quickly on both sides.
❸ Place one pancake on a heatproof dish or baking sheet. Cover with a layer of tomatoes and courgettes. Sprinkle over the walnut mixture.
❹ Cover it with another pancake and continue to repeat layers until

all the pancakes have been used, finishing with a pancake. Top with sliced cheese and bake at 190C/375F/Gas 5 for about 35 minutes until heated through. Serve with the Parmesan cheese.

Spiced potato pancakes

Makes 16

1kg/2lb potatoes, coarsely grated

25g/1oz plain flour

2 tsp baking powder

2 eggs

$\frac{1}{4}$ tsp turmeric

seasoning

1 tsp coriander seeds, roughly crushed

2 tbsp sesame seeds

❶ Dry the potatoes between several sheets of kitchen paper.
❷ Sift the flour and baking powder into a large bowl. Add the eggs, turmeric and seasoning and whisk until smooth.
❸ Add the potatoes, coriander and sesame seeds, and mix together.

❹ Heat a little oil in a heavy-based frying pan. Drop tablespoonfuls of the potato mixture, well spaced apart, into the hot frying pan. Cook for 5 minutes, turning once, until the pancakes are golden and cooked through.
❺ Remove with a palette knife, drain on kitchen paper and keep hot while you cook remaining mixture. Serve at once with grilled bacon and tomatoes for a light lunch.

Scotch pancakes

Try adding the grated rind of one orange and 50g/2oz sultanas or two pieces of drained and chopped stem ginger for variety.

Makes 16

100g/4oz self-raising flour

25g/1oz caster sugar

1 egg

150ml/$\frac{1}{4}$ pint milk

❶ Sift the flour into a bowl. Stir in the sugar and add the egg. Gradually whisk in the milk to make a smooth, thick batter.

3 Using a palette knife, flip over the pancake and cook the other side until it is golden brown. Slide the pancake out of the pan. Heat a little more oil and cook the remaining batter.

4 If you like traditional lemon pancakes, simply squeeze a little lemon juice over each pancake and sprinkle with caster sugar to taste. Roll up each pancake and serve while still warm.

5 If preparing in advance, interleave each pancake with greaseproof paper. Reheat in the microwave for about 2 minutes or cover and place on a plate over a pan of simmering water until heated through.

2 Heat a griddle or heavy-based frying pan and brush with oil.
3 Drop tablespoonfuls of the mixture, well spaced apart, on to the hot griddle or frying pan. Cook until bubbles just appear on the surfaces and the undersides are golden. Turn over and cook until the bases are golden.
4 Transfer pancakes and keep warm in a napkin while you cook remainder. Serve immediately with butter and honey.

Smoked salmon blinis

Serves 6 (makes 24)

75g/3oz self-raising flour

75g/3oz self-raising wholemeal flour

seasoning

2 eggs, separated

25g/1oz butter, melted

200ml/$\frac{1}{3}$ pint of milk

225g/8oz smoked salmon, in strips

juice of $\frac{1}{2}$ lemon

300ml/$\frac{1}{2}$ pint soured cream

4 tsp smoked cod's roe

1 Sift the flours and seasoning into a bowl and tip in the bran from the sieve.
2 Add yolks and butter, then gradually whisk in milk to form a thick batter.
3 Whisk egg whites until stiff and fold into the batter. Heat a griddle or heavy frying pan and brush with oil.
4 Cook tablespoonfuls of mixture until bubbles just appear, then turn over and cook until golden. Keep the blinis warm while you cook remaining mixture.
5 Sprinkle salmon with lemon juice and black pepper. Arrange salmon on blinis, then top with soured cream and cod's roe.

Flambéed crêpes

Makes 8

50g/2oz butter

1 orange, rind and juice

1 lemon, rind and juice

2 passion fruit

50g/2oz caster sugar

50ml/$\frac{1}{4}$ pint orange juice

8 prepared pancakes (see steps above)

3 tbsp orange liqueur or brandy

1 Melt butter in a frying pan. Add orange rind and juice, lemon rind and juice, scooped out flesh from passion fruit and sugar to the pan.
2 Dip eight prepared pancakes in mixture and fold into quarters. Arrange in pan.
3 Add 3 tablespoons of orange liqueur or brandy. Heat gently and light with a taper before serving.

DEEP-FRIED BATTERS

A perfect coating for fish, fruit and vegetables. Half-fill a large, heavy-based pan with light vegetable or soya oil and heat. (Test by spooning in a little batter – it should rise to the surface and sizzle).

50g/2oz self-raising flour
50g/2oz cornflour
pinch of salt
1 tbsp oil
1 egg white

❶ Sift the flours and salt into a large bowl. Make a well in the centre. Mix the oil with 150ml/$\frac{1}{4}$ pint cold water and pour most of this mixture into the well.

❷ Beat mixture, gradually incorporating the flour to form a batter. Beat in remaining water until smooth. Cover and leave to stand for about 1 hour.

Fruit in crispy batter

Serves 4–6

$\frac{1}{2}$ **small pineapple**
1 firm, ripe mango
2 bananas, peeled
1 tbsp plain flour
1 quantity basic Deep-fried batter (see above)
oil, for deep frying
25g/1oz caster sugar
$\frac{1}{2}$ **tsp ground cinnamon**
whipped cream, to serve

❶ Slice pineapple and remove the skin and core. Cut through mango, either side of the flat stone, peel skin and thickly slice the flesh. Cut bananas into 5cm/2in lengths.

❷ Coat each piece of fruit lightly in flour, dip in batter and deep fry a few at a time until crisp. Drain well on kitchen paper.
❸ Mix sugar and cinnamon and lightly dust fruits. Serve warm with whipped cream.

❸ Whisk egg white in a grease-free bowl until 'peaking'. Fold a quarter of egg white into the batter with a metal spoon. Fold in the remainder.

❹ Cut pieces of skinned and boned fish to the required size. Season some flour with salt and pepper and use this mixture to coat the fish.

❺ Dip fish pieces in batter and fry a few at a time in hot oil for 2–3 minutes until crisp and beginning to colour. Drain on kitchen paper before serving.

Tempura

Serves 4

50g/2oz self-raising flour

50g/2oz cornflour

pinch of salt

1 egg, beaten

1 ice cube

225g/8oz whole prawns

1 onion, halved and sliced

1 red pepper, cut into thick strips

2 small carrots, cut into thin sticks

50g/2oz mangetout, trimmed

50g/2oz mushrooms, halved

oil, for deep frying

FOR THE SAUCE

150ml/$\frac{1}{4}$ pint stock

1 tbsp soy sauce

1 tsp sugar

2 tbsp dry sherry or rice wine

❶ Sift the flours and salt into a bowl. Mix the egg with 175ml/6fl oz cold water and add to the bowl, whisking thoroughly. Stir in the ice cube.

❷ Peel the prawns, leaving the tails on. Press a cocktail stick through onion slices to secure.

❸ Dip prawns and vegetables in batter and deep fry for 30 seconds.

❹ Combine sauce ingredients together and serve with tempura.

From left: Fruit in crispy batter and Tempura

BASIC PUDDING BATTER

Yorkshire pudding, Toad-in-the-hole and sweet French Clafoutis are three of the most delicious dishes which are made with batter. For well risen Yorkshire pud, make sure the oven is at the correct temperature and always preheat the fat in the roasting tin.

Makes 12 small puddings

100g/4oz plain flour

pinch of salt

2 eggs

300ml/½ pint milk

❶ Sift flour and salt and break egg into centre. Beat milk in gradually till smooth. To add extra flavour to Yorkshire pudding, try adding 1 tablespoon of coarse mustard and a small handful of fresh chopped herbs.

❷ Preheat the oven to 220C/ 425F/ Gas 7. Add a knob of lard to the roasting tin, or Yorkshire pudding tin sections, and place in the oven for about 5 minutes until it has melted and is very hot.

Plum clafoutis

Serves 6

4 eggs

100g/4oz caster sugar

1 tsp vanilla essence

2 tbsp brandy

50g/2oz plain flour

300ml/½ pint milk

butter, for greasing

750g/1½lb plums

icing sugar, for dusting

cream, to serve

❶ Preheat the oven to 180C/ 350F/Gas 4. Beat together the eggs, sugar, vanilla essence and brandy until foamy.
❷ Beat in the flour, then the milk.
❸ Butter a shallow, ovenproof dish. Prick the plums and arrange them in the dish.

❹ Pour the batter around the plums and bake for about 1 hour until just firm, or until a skewer inserted into the centre comes out clean. Dust with icing sugar and serve with cream. A clafoutis works equally well with apricots, cherries and other firm fruits.

3 Immediately pour the batter over the fat and return to the oven. Cook, without opening the oven door, for 30–40 minutes for a large pudding, or about 20 minutes for smaller, individual ones.

4 To make sweet fruit popovers, add one tablespoon of caster sugar and a few drops of vanilla or almond essence to basic batter. After melting fat in the tin sections, pour in the batter to half fill each one.

5 Quickly add several slices of apple or pear, or small whole fruits. Return to the oven and bake for about 20 minutes until well risen and golden brown. Serve dusted with icing sugar.

Toad-in-the-hole

Serves 4

450g/1lb pork sausages

1 onion, chopped

2 garlic cloves, crushed

2 tbsp oil

1 tbsp chopped fresh sage

1 quantity basic pudding batter (see above left)

sage leaves, to garnish

1 Preheat the oven to 220C/ 425F/Gas 7. Fry the sausages, onion and garlic in the oil until they just begin to colour.

2 Transfer them to a large, shallow ovenproof dish, or four small dishes. Bake for 3 minutes.

3 Add sage to batter and pour over the sausages. Bake for 40–45 minutes until well risen and golden. Garnish with sage leaves.

From left: Plum clafoutis, Sweet fruit popovers (recipe above, step 4) and Toad-in-the-hole

Pastry

For shortcrust, choux, rough puff, pâte sucrée or suet pastry, the art of pastry-making is guaranteed to be successful with our easy steps.

Broccoli and bacon quiche

Serves 6

1 quantity shortcrust pastry (see page 118)

100g/4oz back bacon, rind removed and cut into strips

1 tbsp vegetable oil

1 medium onion, chopped

275g/10oz broccoli

75g/3oz Cheddar cheese, grated

2 eggs

200ml/$\frac{1}{3}$ pint milk

seasoning

❶ Preheat oven to 200C/400F/Gas 6. Lightly grease a 20cm/8in flan ring or tin and put on a baking sheet. Roll out your home-made shortcrust pastry to form a 30.5cm/12 in circle. Line tin with the pastry, pressing it against the sides. Trim top edge with a knife. Allow the case to rest for 30 minutes.

❷ Bake blind before adding filling, this helps give a nice crisp case: cover base and sides of the pastry case with a circle of greaseproof paper and fill with dried beans or rice. Bake for 25–30 minutes.

❸ Remove beans and paper. Turn oven down to 180C/350F/Gas 4. Fry bacon in vegetable oil until crisp, add onion, cover and soften for 3–4 minutes. Turn out into the previously baked pastry case. Cut the broccoli into bite-sized pieces and cook for 3–4 minutes. It should still be fairly crunchy – be careful not to let overcook.

❹ Sprinkle 50g/2oz of cheese over bacon and onions, followed by broccoli.

❺ Beat the eggs together with milk and season well. Pour into case, sprinkle with remaining cheese, bake for 20–25 minutes.

From left: Broccoli and bacon quiche and Apple and rhubarb pie with a sugar lattice crust (recipe page 118)

SHORTCRUST PASTRY

Follow these simple steps to successfully make your own shortcrust pastry. Made with or without sugar, shortcrust pastry can be used to make sumptuous quiches, flans and pies.

Makes 350g/12oz

225g/8oz flour

1 large pinch of salt

1 tbsp caster sugar (for sweet shortcrust)

100g/4oz cool butter or margarine, cut into even pieces

❶ Sift flour, salt and sugar (if using) into a large mixing bowl. Add the butter or margarine. Run your hands under the cold tap to cool, and dry.

❷ Rub fat into flour between finger tips until it resembles large breadcrumbs. Trickle the mixture between your fingers to incorporate air.

❸ Add 4 tablespoons of cold water (ice cold if possible) to the crumbly mixture and stir with a table knife until pastry ingredients are loosely combined.

❹ Turn contents of bowl out on to lightly floured work surface and press mixture together with fingers to form an even pastry. Avoid over-mixing to retain lightness.

❺ Wrap pastry neatly in clingfilm and allow to rest in fridge for at least 1 hour before using. This will help to prevent possible shrinkage.

Apple and rhubarb pie with a sugar lattice crust

Serves 6

1 quantity sweet Shortcrust pastry

900g/2lb cooking apples, peeled, cored and chopped

225g/8oz rhubarb, peeled and chopped

finely grated zest and juice of 1 orange

75g/3oz caster sugar

1 tsp ground ginger

1 egg white

sugar for glazing

❶ Preheat oven to 200C/400F/Gas 6. Place apple and rhubarb in a 1.1litre/2 pint pie dish. Combine orange zest with sugar and ginger. Sprinkle over fruit; add orange juice.

❷ Roll out two-thirds of pastry on a lightly floured surface to a thickness of 3mm/$\frac{1}{8}$in. Moisten edges of pie dish with water, cover with the pastry to make a lid and trim.

❸ Roll out trimmings, brush with beaten egg white and dredge with caster sugar. Cut pastry into 2cm/$\frac{3}{4}$in strips. Moisten pie top and create a lattice pattern by overlaying the strips on the lid. Roll out remaining third of pastry, cut into leaves and make an attractive border. Allow the pie to rest for 30 minutes, then bake for 40–45 minutes until crisp and golden. Serve with lashings of hot custard.

Spicy date triangles

Serves 4

100g/4oz dates, chopped

175g/6oz Cox's Pippins, cored, sliced and chopped

40g/1½oz light muscovado sugar

½ tsp ground cinnamon

6 sheets filo pastry, 36 × 18cm/14 × 6¾in, cut in half

melted butter, for glazing

icing sugar, for dusting

❶ Preheat oven to 200C/400F/ Gas 6. Mix dates, apple, sugar and cinnamon. Place a spoonful of mixture at the top corner of each strip of pastry. Fold over one corner of pastry to form a triangle shape. Fold triangle over down the length of strip.

❷ Brush with melted butter and bake on a greased baking sheet for 12 minutes until crisp and golden. Dredge with icing sugar and serve.

Pear and walnut galette

Serves 6

100g/4oz unsalted butter

100g/4oz clear honey

275g/10oz ready-made filo pastry

50g/2oz walnut pieces, chopped

675g/1½lb pears, peeled, cored and thinly sliced

2 tbsp each clear honey and brandy, to finish

❶ Preheat the oven to 220C/ 425F/Gas 7. Melt together the butter and honey. Cut the sheets of filo pastry in half and cover with a damp tea towel to prevent them from drying out.

❷ Line a 23cm/9in *moule à manqué* tin with one piece of pastry and brush with the butter and honey mixture. Repeat this process with two more pieces of pastry. Sprinkle over half of the walnut pieces, then repeat the pastry and butter layers three more times.

❸ Arrange the pears over the pastry, leaving a 1cm/½in border. Drizzle over 2 tablespoons of the butter and honey mixture. Top with two more layers of pastry and butter. Sprinkle over the remaining chopped walnuts. Fold in the pastry edges and brush with the butter and honey mixture. Scrunch up the remaining four pieces of pastry and arrange over the top.

❹ Drizzle over any remaining butter and honey mixture. Bake for 20 minutes until crisp and golden. To finish, warm together the honey and brandy and pour it over the galette. Serve warm at once.

Profiteroles with chocolate sauce

Serves 4–6

1 quantity Choux pastry (see right)

300ml/½ pint double cream, whipped

200g/7oz plain chocolate

25g/1oz butter

25g/1oz golden syrup

2 tbsp double cream

❶ Using a piping bag, pipe whipped cream through the slit in the base of each bun. Pile on to a serving plate.

❷ Melt the chocolate, butter and syrup in a pan. Stir in the 2 tablespoons of cream and, just before serving, pour over the sauce.

Choux pastry

65g/2½oz plain flour, sifted

50g/2oz butter or margarine

150ml/¼ pint water

2 eggs, beaten

❶ Preheat oven to 220C/425F/ Gas 7. Sift the flour on to a sheet of greaseproof paper. Gently heat fat and water until melted. Bring to the boil, remove from the heat.

❷ Tip the flour into the hot butter/water mixture and beat thoroughly with a wooden spoon until the dough binds together. Then return the pan to the heat.

❸ Beat until the mixture forms a smooth shiny ball and leaves sides of the pan. Cool for 2 or 3 minutes – otherwise, the eggs will cook before they are blended.

❹ Gradually beat in the eggs. Continue beating until the mixture becomes shiny and smooth, but don't overbeat. Place a 2.5cm/1in plain nozzle in a piping bag.

❺ For profiteroles, pipe walnut-sized rounds on to baking sheets. For eclairs, pipe 5cm/2in lengths onto baking sheets. Bake until risen, golden and crisp – 15–20 minutes. Slit the bases to let steam escape. Crisp in oven for a minute or two. Or store in airtight container for 1–2 days/freeze up to one month. Re-crisp in hot oven.

Cheese beignets

Add 50g/2oz grated Cheddar cheese to the paste, and season with salt, pepper and a little cayenne pepper. Deep fry in hot oil and serve the beignets hot with grated Parmesan scattered over.

ROUGH PUFF PASTRY

Better than shortcrust, tastier than frozen puff pastry, rough puff is easy to make and promises golden layers of flaky buttery pastry. Use for sweet and savoury pie coverings, strawberry mille-feuilles, mince pies and sausage rolls.

Use rough puff pastry when you want a light flaky result but not if you want a good rise, when making vol au vents, for example (for them, use puff pastry, best bought frozen as making it is a lengthy process). When rolling out, try not to stretch the pastry – otherwise it will shrink back when you bake it. Give short, sharp rolls in the same direction so you get an even rise. Always chill the pastry after rolling and doing any necessary shaping and before baking to prevent shrinkage.

Makes 450g/1lb

250g/9oz plain flour

generous pinch of salt

175g/6oz cool butter, cut into even pieces

125ml/4fl oz cold water

❶ Sift flour and salt together into a large mixing bowl. Toss butter lightly into flour and break into thumbnail-sized pieces.

Lamb Wellington

Serves 6

1 tbsp vegetable oil

1.1kg/2¼ lb loin of lamb, boned, trimmed of all fat and tied

seasoning

225g/8oz button mushrooms, sliced

1 tsp thyme

1 garlic clove, crushed

1 quantity Rough puff pastry (see above)

175g/6oz fine liver sausage

3 tbsp milk

1 egg, beaten

FOR THE GRAVY

5½ tbsp red wine

300ml/½ pint beef stock

1 tbsp cornflour

1 tsp wine vinegar

❶ Preheat oven to 220C/425F/ Gas 7. Heat oil in a roasting tin directly over heat, season and brown meat on all sides. Roast in oven for 15 minutes. Pour excess fat into a saucepan and save sediment for gravy. Turn oven down to 200C/400F/Gas 6.
❷ Add mushrooms, thyme and garlic to fat and fry for 4–5 minutes until soft. Season, set aside.

❸ Roll two-thirds of pastry to a rectangle 20 × 30cm/8 × 12in. Soften liver sausage with milk; spread to 4cm/1½in of edges. Cover with mushrooms, untie meat, place in centre. Cut out corner squares, brush with egg, enclose meat; turn over on to a baking sheet. Make leaves with trimmings. Brush with egg; leave to rest for 30 minutes. Bake for 30–35 minutes (rare), 45 minutes (medium).
❹ For gravy, pour wine into roasting tin, bring to boil. Add stock and simmer. Mix cornflour with 2 tablespoons of cold water and stir into sauce. Season and add vinegar to sharpen the taste.

Strawberry mille feuilles

Serves 6

1 quantity Rough puff pastry (see above)

3 tbsp strawberry jam

450ml/¾ pint double cream, lightly whipped

1 tbsp caster sugar

750g/1½lb strawberries, halved

50g/2oz flaked almonds, toasted

❶ Divide pastry in half. Roll each half into a rectangle measuring about 25 × 30cm/10 × 12in. Transfer to two baking sheets. Prick all over with a fork and leave to rest in a cool place for 30 minutes. Meanwhile preheat oven to 200C/400F/Gas 6 and bake one tray at a time in the centre of the oven for 25–30 minutes until light and crisp. Cut each piece in half and trim to make four even pieces.
❷ When it is cool, spread three pieces of pastry with strawberry jam, top the first piece with some of the whipped cream, sweetened with caster sugar, and top with strawberries. Repeat with second and third pieces, place them on top of each other, and top the stack with plain rectangle.
❸ Cover sides of the completed mille feuilles with flaked almonds and decorate top with sliced strawberries and cream.

Right: Strawberry mille feuille

❷ Add water and stir loosely into an even dough with a table knife. Turn out onto floured work surface and press mixture together with fingers until it forms a coherent dough. Don't knead, just gather.

❸ To incorporate even layers, roll pastry into a long rectangle and fold into three as if it were a business letter, folding the bottom third up and the top third down over that.

❹ Turn so that open ends face north and south, dust with flour and repeat rolling and folding. Wrap pastry in cling-film and allow to rest for 45 minutes before using.

SUET CRUST PASTRY

Perfect suet crust pastry should have a light, spongy texture. Use vegetable suet if possible – it makes a very light and slightly healthier pastry or make suet crust pastry with wholemeal flour and replace 75g/3oz of the flour with 75g/3oz fresh breadcrumbs for a lighter texture.

Makes about 675g/1½ lb
350g/12oz self-raising flour
pinch of salt
175g/6oz shredded suet

❶ Sift the flour and salt into a large mixing bowl and stir in the suet. Gradually mix in about 250–300ml/8–10fl oz cold water until you have formed a soft dough that is not too sticky.

❷ Knead the dough very lightly on a floured work surface and roll out into a large round about 5mm/¼ in thick. Cut a quarter-sized wedge from the dough and set it aside for the lid.

Bacon and Stilton plate pie

Serves 4
½ quantity Suet crust pastry (see above)
1 tbsp olive oil
1 small onion, chopped
100g/4oz back bacon, diced
225g/8oz leeks, thinly sliced
75g/3oz Stilton, crumbled
4 tbsp single cream
seasoning
beaten egg, to glaze

❶ Preheat oven to 220C/425F/Gas 7. Roll out half the pastry and line a 20cm/8 in pie plate. Fry onion and bacon in oil for 5 minutes. Add leeks and cook until soft. Stir in Stilton, cream and seasoning and spoon into the pastry. Top with remaining pastry, seal and brush with egg.
❷ Bake for 15 minutes. Reduce oven to 180C/350F/Gas 4 for 20–25 minutes until golden.

From left: Bacon and Stilton plate pie and Apple pond pudding with custard

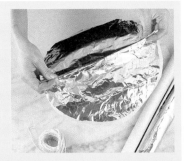

❸ Shape the remaining three-quarters of dough into a cone and then ease it into the pudding basin, leaving an overhang. Press into place and pinch the cut edges together to seal completely.

❹ After filling the pudding, re-roll the remaining dough into a round for the lid, brush the edges with water and place in position. Press the edges together to seal. Trim away any excess.

❺ Cover the pudding basin with buttered greaseproof paper and foil. Make a wide pleat in the middle of both to allow for expansion during cooking. Tie securely with string, leaving enough for a handle. Steam for $3\frac{1}{2}$–4 hours.

Apple pond pudding

Serves 6

1 quantity Suet crust pastry with $\frac{1}{2}$ tsp ground cinnamon and grated rind of 1 lemon (see above)

1 small lemon, well scrubbed

100g/4oz demerara sugar

100g/4oz butter, cubed

350g/12oz cooking apples, cored and sliced

❶ Line a 1.5 litre/$2\frac{1}{2}$ pint pudding basin with three-quarters of the pastry (see steps 2 and 3 above).
❷ Prick the lemon all over with a skewer. Mix together the demerara sugar and butter. Layer the apple slices and butter mixture in the basin, placing the lemon in the centre as you go.
❸ Roll out remaining pastry and use to cover the pudding. Seal and cover with greaseproof paper and foil, as step 5 above. Steam the pudding for $3\frac{1}{2}$–4 hours, topping up pan regularly with boiling water to avoid it boiling dry. Turn out pudding and serve immediately with pouring cream or custard.

PÂTE SUCRÉE

This rich, sweet, short pastry is thin and crisp with a melt-in-the mouth texture; it holds its shape, shrinks very little and does not spread during baking. The key to success is to use butter that is soft, not chilled.

Makes 350–425g/12–15 oz
175g/6oz plain flour
75g/3oz golden caster sugar
75g/3oz butter, at room temperature, cubed
3 egg yolks

❶ Sift the flour on to a cool working surface – marble is ideal, but melamine will do just as well. Make a large well in the centre of the flour and place the sugar, butter and egg yolks in it.

❷ Pinch together the butter, sugar and egg yolks with the fingertips of one hand and work at the ingredients until they resemble very moist scrambled eggs – this gets easier with practice.

Glazed citrus tart

A deliciously sharp refreshing dessert that makes an ideal dessert.

Serves 6
1 orange sliced, 1 lemon sliced and 1 lime sliced
175g/6oz golden caster sugar
1 quantity Pâte sucrée (see above)
75g/3oz butter
grated rind of 1 lemon
2 eggs
150g/5oz ground almonds
85ml/3fl oz double cream

❶ Place the sliced citrus fruit and plenty of water in a pan and simmer for 30 minutes. Drain, pouring 300ml/$\frac{1}{2}$ pint of the liquid into a separate pan. Add 100g/4oz of the sugar to the liquid and stir over a low heat until the sugar dissolves. Pour over the fruit and simmer for a further 5 minutes. Remove the fruit and boil the syrup to reduce by half. Remove the pan from the heat and set aside to allow the syrup to cool.

❷ Preheat oven to 190C/375F/ Gas 5. Roll out pastry to a 25cm/10in circle. Lift over a rolling pin and place pastry over a deep 20cm/8in flan tin. Press pastry against side of tin and trim off excess with a knife. Beat together the butter, remaining sugar and lemon rind. Beat in the eggs, fold in the almonds and cream. Spread into the pastry case.

❸ Bake for about 30–35 minutes until well risen and golden. Leave to cool slightly for the filling to settle, then arrange the sliced citrus fruit on the top and brush with the cooled syrup. Serve the tart warm or cold.

Fruit diamonds

Serves 4
1 quantity Hazelnut pâte sucrée (see above right)
1 small ripe mango, peeled, stoned and diced
300ml/$\frac{1}{2}$ pint crème fraîche
icing sugar and ground cinnamon, for dusting

❶ Preheat the oven to 190C/375F/Gas 5. Roll out the pastry thinly and cut out 12 diamonds measuring 10cm/4in from top to bottom. Bake for 10–12 minutes until golden. Halve four of the diamonds while warm to make eight triangles. Cool on a rack.

❷ Stir the mango into the crème fraîche. Use to sandwich the diamonds. Top with mango mixture and pastry triangles. Dust with icing sugar and cinnamon.

From left: Glazed citrus tart and Fruit diamonds

❸ Gradually work the mixture into the flour, using either your fingers or a round-bladed knife. When all of the flour has been incorporated, form into a ball and knead lightly until smooth.

❹ Wrap the pastry in foil and leave to rest in the fridge for at least 30 minutes. The pâte sucrée can be made the day before, but always allow it to return to room temperature before using it.

Pâte sucrée variations
- **Citrus** – add the finely grated rind of half a lemon, lime or orange to the well in the centre of the flour. Mix as before.
- **Nut** – use 100g/4oz plain flour mixed with 50g/2oz ground, toasted hazelnuts, ground almonds, walnuts or pecan nuts. Make a well in the centre and work in 50g/2oz golden caster sugar, 100g/4oz butter and two egg yolks. Mix together, but be careful not to overmix or the pastry will turn oily.
- **Spicy** – add a large pinch of ground cinnamon, mixed spice, freshly grated nutmeg or finely crushed cardamom seeds.
- **Vanilla** – add ½ teaspoon of vanilla essence with the egg yolks.

Breads

From simple loaves of bread to French recipes for rich buttery brioche and croissants, bread-making is one of the most rewarding cookery skills. There is nothing quite like the taste and aroma of freshly baked bread.

Flowerpot loaves

Makes 6 small loaves

2 tsp dried yeast or 15g/½oz fresh yeast

2 tbsp clear honey

1kg/2lb wholemeal flour

1 tbsp salt

2 tbsp sunflower oil

beaten egg, to glaze

whole or cracked wheat, or coarse oatmeal, to sprinkle

❶ Dissolve yeast with honey in 150ml/¼ pint of hand-hot water. Leave until frothy.

❷ Add yeast to flour, salt and oil in a mixing bowl. Stir in 600ml/ 1 pint of hand-hot water and mix to a dough. Knead on floured surface. Place in bowl, cover and leave to rise in warmth for about 1 hour.

❸ Oil six terracotta pots or two 450g/1lb loaf tins. Divide dough, shape and drop into pots.

❹ Leave to rise above the rim. Preheat oven to 200C/400F/ Gas 6. Brush with beaten egg and sprinkle with grains. Bake for 30 minutes.

Enriched milk plait

Makes 1 large plait

2 tsp dried yeast or 15g/½oz fresh yeast

150ml/¼ pint hand-hot milk

25g/1oz caster sugar

350g/12oz strong plain flour

1 tsp salt

50g/2oz butter or margarine, melted

1 egg, beaten

beaten egg, to glaze

poppy seeds, to sprinkle

❶ Sprinkle dried yeast or crumble fresh yeast into the milk with 1 tsp caster sugar. Stir lightly and leave in a warm place until frothy, about 10–15 minutes.

❷ Sift flour and salt together into a mixing bowl. Add frothy yeast mixture, melted fat, remaining sugar and egg. Mix with a round-bladed knife to make a dough. Knead on a generously floured surface until smooth. Place in a clean bowl, cover with clingfilm and leave to rise in a warm place until double in size. If you have time punch back dough to remove air and leave to rise for a second time. This gives an even lighter, more aerated bread.

❸ Grease a baking sheet. Divide dough into three pieces. Roll into sausage shapes, about 30cm/12in long. Pinch ends together, then plait. Leave to rise on baking sheet until doubled in size. Preheat oven to 200C/400F/Gas 6. Brush with beaten egg and sprinkle with seeds. Bake 40 minutes.

From left: Flowerpot loaves, Enriched milk plait and Basic bread (see overleaf)

BASIC BREAD

Plain flour, preferably strong, is used, but half wholemeal or Granary can be substituted. If cooked loaves don't sound 'hollow' when tapped on the base return to oven without tin for 5–10 minutes.

Makes 1 1kg/2lb loaf or two 450g/1lb loaves

1 tsp caster sugar
2 tsp dried yeast or 15g/$\frac{1}{2}$oz fresh yeast
600g/1lb 6oz strong plain flour
2 tsp salt
beaten egg, to glaze

❶ Place 150ml/$\frac{1}{4}$ pint of hand-hot water in a jug with the sugar. Sprinkle over dried yeast or crumble in fresh yeast. Stir lightly and leave in a warm place for 10–15 minutes until the mixture is frothy.

❷ Sift flour and salt together into a bowl. Add frothy yeast mixture and 300ml/$\frac{1}{2}$ pint of hand-hot water. Stir flour and water mixture with a round-bladed knife until it forms a dough.

Country breads

Try adding cheese, herbs, tomatoes and garlic to this moist, nutty bread.

Makes 2 sticks

2 tsp easy-blend dried yeast
3 tsp salt
350g/12oz wholemeal or Granary flour
450g/1lb strong plain flour
1 tbsp sugar
350ml/12 fl oz hand-hot milk
25g/1oz butter or margarine, melted

❶ Sprinkle yeast and 2 teaspoons of salt over the flours. Stir in sugar, milk, fat and 175ml/6fl oz of hand-hot water. Knead for 10 minutes until firm and elastic.
❷ Place dough in a clean bowl. Cover with oiled clingfilm and leave in a warm place until double in size, about 1 hour. Punch back and leave to rise for 40 minutes.
❸ Knead dough lightly, then roll into two sausage shapes about 38cm/15in long. Place on baking tray, cover with oiled clingfilm and leave to rise. Cut in diagonal slits.

❹ Place a roasting tin, half filled with hot water, in the base of the oven at 220C/425F/Gas 7 to provide steam. Mix 1 teaspoon of salt with 8 tablespoons of hot water. Brush over dough.
❺ Bake for 15 minutes in a separate tin above the steam, then rebrush with the salt mixture. Reduce oven to 190C/375F/Gas 5 and cook for a further 15 minutes. Cool on a wire rack.

Country loaf with tomatoes and garlic

Serves 6–8

1 tsp easy-blend dried yeast
1 tsp salt
175g/6oz wholemeal or Granary flour
225g/8oz strong plain flour
1$\frac{1}{4}$ tsp sugar
175ml/6fl oz hand-hot milk
15g/$\frac{1}{2}$oz butter or margarine, melted
3 tbsp sun-dried tomato purée
3 garlic cloves, crushed
flour, for dusting

❶ Sprinkle yeast and salt over flours. Stir in sugar, milk, fat, tomato purée, garlic and 5$\frac{1}{2}$ tablespoons of hand-hot water. Knead for 10 minutes until firm.
❷ Place dough in a clean bowl. Cover with oiled clingfilm and leave in a warm place until double in size, about 1 hour. Punch back and leave to rise for 40 minutes. Knead lightly, then shape dough into a round loaf.
❸ Using a sharp knife, make several slashes across the top of the loaf, then again across in the opposite direction to make a square pattern.
❹ Half fill a medium roasting tin with hot water and place it in the base of the oven at 220C/425F/Gas 7. Place dough on a greased baking sheet and dust with flour just before baking. Bake for 15 minutes and allow an extra 15 minutes at 190C/375F/Gas 5 until the base of the loaf sounds hollow when it is tapped. If it still sounds doughy, return it to the oven upside down for a few more minutes.

3 Knead on a generously floured surface until smooth, about 10 minutes. Place in a clean bowl and cover with clingfilm. Leave dough to rise in a warm place for about 1 hour until double in size.

4 Punch back dough to release air. Turn out on to a lightly floured surface knead well, and divide in half if making two small loaves. Thoroughly grease one 1kg/2lb or two 450g/1lb loaf tins.

5 Shape dough and place in tin(s). Cover with oiled clingfilm. Leave to rise above rim of tin. Preheat oven to 200C/400F/Gas 6. Brush with egg and bake small loaves for 30 minutes and large for 50 minutes.

Cheese and herb bun loaf

Serves 8

2 tsp easy-blend dried yeast

3 tsp salt

350g/12oz wholemeal or Granary flour

450g/1lb strong plain flour

1 tbsp sugar

350ml/12 fl oz hand-hot milk

25g/1oz butter or margarine, melted

175g/6oz Cheddar cheese, grated

3–4 tbsp chopped fresh thyme

3–4 tbsp chopped fresh parsley

1 Sprinkle the yeast and 2 teaspoons of salt over flours. Stir in sugar, milk, fat and 175ml/6fl oz of hand-hot water. Knead for 10 minutes until firm and elastic.
2 Place dough in a clean bowl. Cover with oiled clingfilm and leave in a warm place until double in size, about 1 hour. Punch back the dough and leave it to rise for 40 minutes.
3 Knead dough lightly. Roll out to a 30cm/12in square and sprinkle with cheese and herbs. Roll up.

4 Cut into eight even-sized slices and place cut sides down in a 30 × 23cm/12 × 9in greased roasting tin. Cover with oiled clingfilm and leave to rise until the dough fills the roasting tin.
5 Place a roasting tin, half filled with hot water in the oven at 220C/425F/Gas 7. Then mix 1 teaspoon of salt with 8 tablespoons hot water and brush it over dough. Bake for 15 minutes and rebrush with salt mixture. Reduce oven to 190C/375F/Gas 5 and bake for 20–30 minutes.

Dinner rolls

Makes 16 rolls

Once risen, punch back Basic bread dough, knead lightly and cut into 16 equal pieces. Shape as:
Plait Cut into three pieces and roll each one into a sausage about 11.5cm/4½in long. Pinch ends together then plait to other end. Pinch ends together securely.
Spiral Roll out to a thin sausage about 23cm/9in long. Roll up loosely.

Cottage loaf Cut off a quarter of dough and roll it into a round. Roll remainder into a round and top with the smaller piece. Press a floured finger through both rounds to make a small hole (but one that is big enough to stay open).
Knot Roll out to a thin sausage about 20cm/8in long. Twist into a knot.
Twist Cut in half and roll each one into a sausage about 13cm/5in long. Lay halves together and twist into a rope.
Trefoil Cut into three pieces and shape each one into a ball. Arrange in triangles with sides just meeting.
Space rolls well apart on greased baking sheets. Cover with greased clingfilm and leave to rise. Brush with beaten egg and sprinkle with sesame, poppy, caraway or fennel seeds. Bake at 200C/400F/Gas 6 for 15 minutes or until golden.

Brioche

Makes 1 large loaf or 10 buns

2 tsp easy-blend dried yeast

350g/12oz strong plain flour

1 tsp salt

4 eggs, beaten

3 tbsp caster sugar

100g/4oz butter, softened

beaten egg, to glaze

❶ If you don't have brioche tins, use two large loaf tins. Sprinkle yeast over the flour and salt. Add eggs, sugar and 4 tablespoons of hand-hot water. Mix to a sticky dough and knead for 10 minutes, flouring hands frequently.

❷ Dot the dough with butter and knead until the butter has been absorbed.

❸ Leave to rise for 1 hour. Punch down to release air and leave to rise again for a further hour.

❹ For a large brioche, shape three-quarters of the dough into a ball and place in a greased brioche tin. Make a depression in the centre with your finger. Shape the remaining dough into a ball and rest it on top.

❺ For a smaller brioche, use small brioche tins, divide dough into 10 pieces and use technique above for each.

❻ Cover loosely with oiled clingfilm and leave for 1 hour until well risen.

❼ Preheat the oven to 200C/400F/Gas 6. Brush dough with egg. Bake a large brioche for 50 minutes, and the small ones for 15 minutes. Cool on a wire rack.

Croissants

Making croissants can be time-consuming, but the results are rewarding. Use easy-blend dried yeast to speed up preparation.

Makes 10

2 tsp easy-blend dried yeast

300g/11oz strong plain flour

1 tsp salt

2 tbsp caster sugar

2 tbsp double cream

100g/4oz butter

beaten egg, to glaze

❶ Sprinkle the yeast over the flour and salt. Stir in sugar, cream and 175ml/6fl oz hand-hot water and mix to a sticky dough. Knead and leave to rise for 2 hours. Flatten butter slightly between clingfilm with a rolling pin.

❷ Working on a lightly floured surface, roll out the dough to a 25cm/10in square. Roll out from the centre to leave a slight dome. Lay the flattened butter over the centre of the dough. Remove clingfilm.

❸ Fold dough corners over the butter to enclose it completely. Roll out to a rectangle, about three times longer than its width. Fold the dough into three and give a quarter turn. Chill for 10 minutes.

❹ Repeat rolling, folding, quarter turning and chilling twice more. Roll out dough thinly to a 38 × 30cm/15 × 12in rectangle. Halve lengthways, then cut into triangles, 13cm/5in on short sides and 15cm/6in to points.

❺ Roll up from short side towards the point and curl ends. Space apart on a greased baking sheet. Cover and leave to rise for $1\frac{1}{2}$ hours. Preheat the oven to 200C/400F/Gas 6. Brush dough with egg. Bake 15–20 minutes. Cool on a wire rack.

Left: Brioche and Croissants

Bagels

Makes 12

2 tsp easy-blend dried yeast

350g/12oz strong plain or wholemeal flour

2 tsp salt

1 tbsp clear honey

100g/4oz strong plain flour

TO FINISH

1 tbsp caster sugar

1 egg white

sesame, poppy or caraway seeds, or finely chopped onion

❶ Sprinkle the yeast over the strong plain or wholemeal flour and salt. Blend the honey with 350ml/12fl oz hand-hot water and add to the bowl. Mix to a sticky dough, using a round-bladed knife. Knead in the strong plain flour on a work surface for 10 minutes or so.

❷ Place in a clean bowl and cover loosely with oiled clingfilm. Leave the dough to rise in a warm place for 1½ hours until double in size.

❸ Punch down dough to release the air bubbles, knead lightly and divide into 12 pieces. Shape each one into a ball and leave to stand for 5 minutes.

❹ Bring 2.25 litres/4 pints of water to the boil with the sugar. Press a hole into each bagel and pull open each one until it is 2.5cm/1in in diameter. Cover loosely with oiled clingfilm and leave for 10 minutes.

❺ Preheat the oven to 230C/450F/Gas 8. Lower the bagels into the boiling water and simmer for 30 seconds on each side. Drain on kitchen paper.

❻ Transfer to greased baking sheets and brush with egg white. Sprinkle with seeds or onion and bake for 10–15 minutes. Cool.

Salt and sesame pretzels

Makes 35

Use half quantity Basic bread dough (see page 128). Once risen, punch back, knead lightly and roll into a thin rectangle, 20cm/8in wide. Cut into thin strips, twist ends together then drop them back over looped ends to give pretzel shapes. Leave to rise on greased baking sheets for 15–20 minutes. Brush with beaten egg and sprinkle with sesame seeds and/or coarse salt. Bake at 200C/400F/Gas 6 for about 10 minutes until golden.

Below: Bagels with onion and sesame seed toppings

Biscuits

Be a smart cookie and bake your own! Biscuit cookery is pure simplicity. The kids just love it as the results are so quick and scrumptious, and there are so many flavours and shapes to choose from.

Lemon garlands

Makes 16

75g/3oz sunflower margarine

75g/3oz soft light brown sugar

75g/3oz wholemeal flour

75g/3oz plain flour

$\frac{1}{4}$ tsp vanilla essence

2 tbsp milk

FOR THE GLACÉ ICING

100g/4oz icing sugar, sifted

4 tsp lemon juice

❶ Preheat the oven to 190C/ 375F/Gas 5. Beat margarine and sugar until fluffy. Sift flours and stir into mixture with vanilla and milk.

❷ Knead lightly and divide into 16 pieces. Divide each of these pieces into eight and roll into balls. Arrange in rings on greased baking sheets and press together to form garlands. Bake for 15–20 minutes until golden. Leave to cool.

❸ Mix the icing sugar with the lemon juice to make smooth, runny icing. Dip biscuit tops in icing.

Peanut butter cookies

Makes 16

50g/2oz sunflower margarine

100g/4oz crunchy peanut butter

75g/3oz soft light brown sugar

100g/4oz self-raising flour

$\frac{1}{2}$ tsp bicarbonate of soda

50g/2oz jumbo oats

50g/2oz unsalted shelled peanuts, chopped

2 tbsp milk

❶ Preheat the oven to 190C/ 375F/Gas 5. Beat together the margarine, peanut butter and sugar until light and fluffy. Mix in the flour, bicarbonate of soda, jumbo oats, peanuts and milk to form a soft dough.

❷ Roll heaped tablespoons of the mixture into balls, and flatten slightly. Arrange well-spaced on greased baking sheets and press down with a fork.

❸ Bake for 15 minutes until golden. Leave to firm on the sheets for a few minutes, then transfer to a rack to cool.

Ginger cookies

Makes about 30

40g/1$\frac{1}{2}$oz black treacle

50g/2oz sunflower margarine

100g/4oz wholemeal flour

$\frac{1}{4}$ tsp bicarbonate of soda

$\frac{1}{2}$ tsp ground ginger

$\frac{1}{4}$ tsp mixed spice

40g/1$\frac{1}{2}$oz soft dark brown sugar

1 tbsp ground hazelnuts

1 egg yolk

❶ Preheat the oven to 190C/ 375F/Gas 5. Melt the treacle and margarine. Cool slightly. Sift the flour, soda, ginger, mixed spice and sugar. Mix in the hazelnuts, cooled mixture and yolk.

❷ Roll out between two sheets of non-stick baking paper. Cut out shapes, place on baking sheets. Bake for 12 minutes until firm. Leave on the sheets to harden.

From left: Anzac biscuits, Coffee spirals, Munchie fruit biscuits, (recipes overleaf) and Ginger cookies, Peanut butter cookies and Lemon garlands

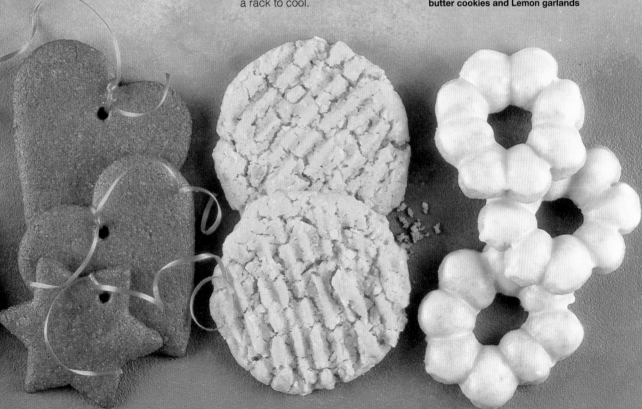

Anzac biscuits

Makes 36
90g/3½oz rolled oats
150g/5oz wholemeal flour
225g/8oz soft light brown sugar
65g/2½oz desiccated coconut
100g/4oz sunflower margarine
2 tbsp clear honey
½ tsp bicarbonate of soda

❶ Preheat the oven to 180C/
350F/Gas 4. Mix together the oats,
flour, sugar and coconut in a large
bowl. Melt the margarine and
honey in a small pan.
❷ Mix the bicarbonate of soda
with 1 tablespoon of water, stir into
margarine and honey. Add to oat
mixture.
❸ Then drop teaspoons of the oat
mixture, well spaced, on to
greased baking sheets. Bake for
about 20 minutes until golden.
Cool on a wire rack.

Coffee spirals

Makes about 24
100g/4oz sunflower margarine
100g/4oz soft light brown sugar
1 egg, beaten
few drops vanilla essence
225g/8oz wholemeal flour
2½ tsp instant coffee powder

❶ Preheat the oven to 190C/
375F/Gas 5. Beat the margarine
and sugar until light. Beat in the
egg and vanilla essence, mix in the
flour to form a soft dough.
❷ Divide the dough in half and
work 2 teaspoons of the coffee into
one half. Roll out each half on
a floured surface to a 20 × 30cm/
8 × 12in rectangle. Place the plain
half on top of the coffee half and
roll them up together.
❸ Wrap in greaseproof paper and
press to form a rectangle. Chill in a
polythene bag for 1 hour. Unwrap,
cut into slices.

❹ Place slices on greased baking
sheets. Bake for 10–15 minutes
until firm. Dust with remaining
coffee and cool on a rack.

Munchy fruit biscuits

Makes 32
150g/5oz of branflakes and dried
fruit-based cereal
90g/3½oz desiccated coconut
100g/4oz soft light brown sugar
175g/6oz sultanas
100g/4oz each ready-to-eat
dried figs and ready-to-eat
apricots, chopped
150g/5oz self-raising wholemeal
flour
175g/6oz sunflower margarine
2 eggs, beaten

❶ Preheat the oven to 190C/375F/
Gas 5. Mix together cereal,
coconut, sugar, dried fruits and
flour. Melt the margarine in a pan.
Cool. Stir into mixture with the
eggs.
❷ Shape into rounds, press flat.
Place on greased baking sheets
and bake for 10 minutes until
golden. Leave for 2 minutes. Cool
on a wire rack.

Sesame squares

Makes about 35
75g/3oz sunflower margarine
175g/6oz plain flour
75g/3oz Gruyère, grated
1 egg, beaten
2 tbsp sesame seeds

❶ Preheat the oven to 190C/375F/
Gas 5. Beat together the
margarine, flour, cheese and half
of the egg, then knead lightly to
form a soft dough. Roll out thinly on
a lightly floured surface and cut
into 5cm/2in squares, using a
sharp knife.
❷ Mark the tops of the squares in
a criss-cross style pattern with the
back of a knife, brush with the
remaining beaten egg and sprinkle
with sesame seeds.
❸ Bake on a greased baking
sheet for 12–15 minutes until
golden. Cool.

**From left: Sesame squares, Cheesy
almond biscuits and Twisted curry
snacks**

Cheesy almond biscuits

Makes 20

75g/3oz sunflower margarine

175g/6oz plain flour

75g/3oz Edam, finely grated

1 egg, separated

4 tbsp grated Parmesan

4 tbsp ground almonds

FOR THE FILLING

15g/½oz sunflower margarine

1 tbsp plain flour

150ml/¼ pint milk

½ tsp wholegrain mustard

seasoning

❶ Preheat oven to 190C/375F/ Gas 5. Beat margarine, flour, Edam and yolk. Knead lightly, roll out thinly and cut 40 rounds using a 5cm/2in fluted cutter. Cut out the centres of 20 rounds with a 2.5cm/1in round cutter.
❷ Mix Parmesan and almonds.

Brush rings with egg white; sprinkle on almond mixture. Bake biscuits on greased baking sheets until golden. Cool on a wire rack.
❸ Melt margarine, add flour and cook for 1 minute. Gradually add milk and boil until thick, stirring. Add mustard and seasoning. Cool. Use to sandwich biscuits.

Twisted curry sticks

Makes 40

2 × 20cm/8in square ready-made sheets frozen puff pastry, thawed

4 tbsp olive oil

2 tsp curry powder

pinch of salt

❶ Preheat the oven to 220C/425F/Gas 7. Cut the puff pastry into strips, 5mm/¼ wide and 10cm/4in long. Twist the strips together in pairs, then brush with the olive oil and sprinkle with the curry powder and salt.
❷ Arrange on a greased baking sheet and bake for 10– 15 minutes until golden brown and crisp. Cool on a wire rack.

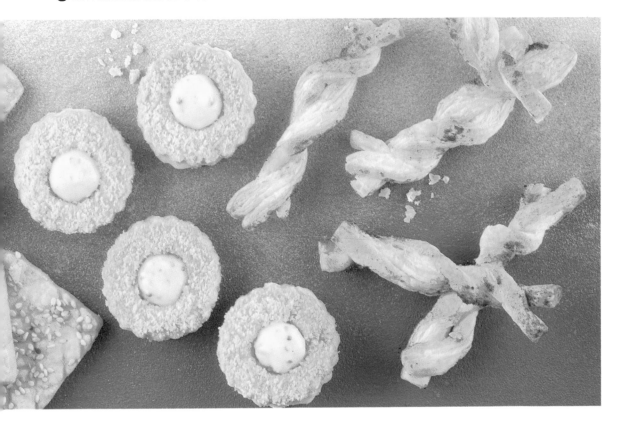

Blueberry slices

Makes 15

100g/4oz blueberries

100g/4oz sunflower margarine

100g/4oz soft light brown sugar

2 eggs, plus 1 yolk, beaten

150g/5oz self-raising wholemeal flour

$\frac{1}{2}$ tsp ground cinnamon

2 tbsp demerara sugar

❶ Preheat the oven to 180C/ 350F/Gas 4. Chop the blueberries roughly. Beat the margarine and sugar until light and fluffy; beat in the eggs a little at a time. Sift together the flour and cinnamon and fold into the mixture. Fold in blueberries.

❷ Spread mixture into a greased and lined 18 × 28cm/7 × 11in tin. Sprinkle with the demerara sugar and bake in the oven for about 35 minutes or until golden brown and firm to the touch.

❸ Turn out on to a wire rack and leave to cool before cutting into thick slices.

Fruit and nut bars

Makes 16

90g/3$\frac{1}{2}$oz rolled oats

100g/4oz dried pears, chopped

75g/3oz self-raising wholemeal flour

50g/2oz light muscovado sugar

50g/2oz roasted hazelnuts

50g/2oz plain chocolate drops

150g/5oz sunflower margarine

5 tbsp clear honey

❶ Preheat the oven to 190C/ 375F/Gas 5. Mix together the oats, pears, flour, sugar, hazelnuts and half of the chocolate. Melt the margarine and honey in a pan and quickly stir into the dry ingredients.

❷ Press the mixture into a greased and lined 18 × 28cm/7 × 11in tin and bake for 15–20 minutes until golden. Leave to cool in the tin, then cut into bars.

❸ Melt the remaining chocolate, drizzle in fine lines over the bars and leave to set.

From left: Blueberry slices, Fruit and nut bars, Date and coconut diamonds, Soft fruit crackles, Muesli munch and Chocolate raisin brownies

Date and coconut diamonds

Makes 15

65g/2$\frac{1}{2}$oz stoned dates, chopped

rind and juice of 2 oranges

75g/3oz sunflower margarine

100g/4oz light muscovado sugar

1 egg, beaten

50g/2oz self-raising wholemeal flour

100g/4oz plain flour

FOR THE TOPPING

65ml/2$\frac{1}{2}$fl oz clear honey

175g/6oz desiccated coconut

2 eggs, beaten

❶ Preheat the oven to 180C/ 350F/Gas 4. Tip the dates, orange rind and juice into a small pan and cook gently until the dates are soft and pulpy. Cool.

❷ Beat the margarine and sugar, then beat in the egg. Sift together the flours and fold into the mixture. Spread into a greased and lined 18 × 28cm/7 × 11in tin.

❸ Spread the date mixture over the base. Stir the honey and coconut into the eggs, spoon over the date mixture and spread evenly. Bake for about 45 minutes until golden brown. Leave to cool in the tin, then cut into diamond shapes.

Soft fruit crackles

These are so scrummy, yet to make them is simplicity itself – they're not even baked, just chilled in the fridge until firm.

Makes about 15

2 tbsp each sesame, sunflower and pumpkin seeds

350g/12oz dried fruit salad

100g/4oz sultanas

3 tbsp orange juice

1 tbsp clear honey

25g/1oz puffed rice cereal

❶ Place the sesame seeds, sunflower seeds, pumpkin seeds, the dried fruits, orange juice and honey in a food processor and blend until you achieve a smooth paste. Tip the mixture into a bowl and stir in the puffed rice cereal.
❷ Spread the mixture into an 18 × 28cm/7 × 11in tin which has been lined with non-stick baking paper and press the mixture down evenly using a palette knife. Chill in the fridge for at least 1 hour, then cut it into about 15 triangles.

Muesli munch

Makes 12

100g/4oz ready-to-eat dried apricots, chopped

50g/2oz sultanas

175g/6oz self-raising wholemeal flour

225g/8oz toasted oat cereal

175g/6oz demerara sugar

175g/6oz sunflower margarine

❶ Preheat the oven to 180C/ 350F/Gas 4. Place the apricots in a small pan with 6 tablespoons of water and simmer gently for 5 minutes until soft. Cool.
❷ In a large bowl, mix together the flour, oat cereal and sugar, then work in the margarine until crumbly. Spoon half of this into a separate bowl and mix in the cooked apricots and sultanas.
❸ Spread half of the remaining mixture into a greased and lined 18 × 28cm/7 × 11in tin. Spread the apricot mixture on top and cover with the remaining crumble.
❹ Press down the mixture using a palette knife, then bake for 35–45 minutes until golden brown. Cool in tin, then cut into squares.

Chocolate raisin brownies

Makes 15

100g/4oz sunflower margarine

175g/6oz plain chocolate

225g/8oz soft light brown sugar

1 tsp vanilla essence

2 eggs, beaten

175g/6oz wholemeal flour

50g/2oz pecan nuts, chopped

100g/4oz raisins

❶ Preheat the oven to 180C/ 350F/Gas 4. Melt the sunflower margarine and plain chocolate in a large bowl. Stir in the brown sugar and vanilla essence, then add the eggs, flour, nuts and raisins.
❷ Pour the mixture into a greased and lined 18 × 28cm/7 × 11in tin and bake for about 30 minutes. Leave to cool completely in the tin before cutting it into squares.

PETITS FOURS

Marzipan whirls

Makes about 30

50g/2oz sunflower margarine
25g/1oz soft light brown sugar
50g/2oz marzipan
1 egg yolk
1 tbsp milk
few drops of almond essence
150g/5oz plain flour
6 tbsp reduced sugar raspberry
jam

❶ Preheat oven to 200C/400F/
Gas 6. Blend together the
margarine, sugar, marzipan, yolk,
milk and almond essence in a food
processor until soft and creamy,
then quickly mix in the flour.
❷ Tip the mixture into a large
piping bag fitted with a medium
size star nozzle and pipe the
mixture in 2.5cm/1in rounds on a
greased baking sheet. Then pipe a
ring on top around the edge of
each base.
❸ Bake the whirls for
10–15 minutes until they turn a
golden brown colour. Leave to cool
slightly, then transfer them to a wire
rack. When quite cold, spoon a
little raspberry jam into the centre
of each whirl.

Nutty petits fours

Makes 30

25g/1oz shelled pistachio nuts
100g/4oz ground hazelnuts
75g/3oz soft light brown sugar
25g/1oz cornflour
25g/1oz sunflower margarine,
melted
1 tbsp soured cream
1 egg, beaten
icing sugar, to decorate

❶ Preheat the oven to 190C/
375F/Gas 5. Soak the pistachio
nuts in boiling water for a few
minutes, drain and peel off the
skins. Chop finely and set aside.
❷ Mix the hazelnuts, brown sugar
and cornflour. Blend in the
margarine, cream, egg and
2 teaspoons of water.
❸ Spoon into 30 doubled paper
petit four cases and arrange on a
baking sheet. Sprinkle with
pistachios and icing sugar.
❹ Bake for 15–20 minutes until
risen and firm to the touch. Cool
on a wire rack.

Rocky chocs

Makes about 40

25g/1oz plain chocolate
50g/2oz ground hazelnuts
40g/1½oz wholemeal semolina
75g/3oz icing sugar
40g/1½oz soft light brown sugar
2 tsp clear honey
1 egg white

❶ Preheat the oven to 220C/
425F/Gas 7. Melt the chocolate
in a small bowl set over hot water.
Mix in the hazelnuts, semolina,
40g/1½oz of the icing sugar, the soft
brown sugar, honey and egg white
to form a soft dough.
❷ Drop rough teaspoons of the
mixture on to greased baking
sheets and bake for
8–10 minutes until set. Mix the
remaining icing sugar with a little
warm water to make a runny icing.
❸ Transfer the biscuits to wire
racks as soon as you remove them
from the oven and quickly drizzle
with the icing while they are still
warm. Leave to cool.

**From left: Rocky chocs, Nutty petits
fours, Marzipan whirls, Chocolate date
chips, Filo pastry plums and Cherry
almond curls**

Chocolate date chips

Makes 24
100g/4oz stoned dates, chopped
50g/2oz self-raising wholemeal flour
75g/3oz plain chocolate, broken into pieces
75g/3oz rolled oats
50g/2oz soft light brown sugar
75g/3oz sunflower margarine

❶ Preheat the oven to 190C/ 375F/Gas 5. Place the dates and 2 teaspoons of the flour in a small pan with 3 tablespoons of water and cook gently for 5 minutes until soft. Add the chocolate and stir until melted, then leave to cool.
❷ Mix the remaining flour with the oats and sugar and rub in the margarine. Mix half of the crumble mixture with the chocolate mixture and spread it evenly in the base of a greased and lined 18cm/7in square cake tin.
❸ Sprinkle the remaining crumble mixture on top and press down firmly with a palette knife. Bake for about 15 minutes until the topping turns a golden brown colour, then leave to cool in the tin. When completely cold, cut the mixture into 24 chip shapes and serve.

Filo pastry plums

Makes 16
25g/1oz ground almonds
25g/1oz soft light brown sugar
$\frac{1}{2}$ egg white
2 plums, halved and stoned
2 20 × 40cm/8 × 16in sheets filo pastry
25g/1oz butter, melted
2 tbsp chopped hazelnuts
icing sugar, to decorate

❶ Preheat the oven to 200C/ 400F/Gas 6. Mix together the almonds and brown sugar, then stir in the egg white. Cut each halved plum into four, then spread with a little of the almond mixture.
❷ Cut pastry into sixteen 10cm/4in squares and then cover with a damp cloth to keep them soft. Wrap each plum in two squares of pastry, twisting the corners together at the top.
❸ Brush the wrapped plums with the butter and place on a baking sheet. Sprinkle the hazelnuts on top and bake for 8–10 minutes until crisp and golden brown. Dust with icing sugar and serve warm, or leave to cool on a wire rack. (Eat these petits fours the same day.)

Cherry almond curls

Makes about 30
40g/1$\frac{1}{2}$oz sunflower margarine
40g/1$\frac{1}{2}$oz soft light brown sugar
25g/1oz wholemeal flour
15g/$\frac{1}{2}$oz flaked almonds
25g/1oz glacé cherries, finely chopped
15g/$\frac{1}{2}$oz cornflakes, crushed

❶ Preheat the oven to 200C/ 400F/Gas 6. Beat together the margarine and sugar until light and fluffy, then stir in the flour, almonds and cherries.
❷ Drop 6 half teaspoons of the mixture, well spaced, onto a greased baking sheet. Press flat and sprinkle on cornflakes, pressing them into mixture. Bake for 5–7 minutes until they have spread thinly and are golden.
❸ Leave to firm for a few seconds, then remove from the baking sheet, one at a time, with a palette knife and drape over a small rolling pin or broom handle. (Wrap a broom handle with non-stick baking paper before draping over biscuits.) Leave until cool and crisp. Repeat the process with remaining mixture.

Cakes

Have your cake and eat it too with this guide to the art of cake-making. Here are the most basic and the most beautiful cakes, with lots of 'quick and tasty' flavour variations to try.

Basic creamed cake

Serves 8

This traditional cake mixture can be served simply as a Victorian sandwich, or dressed up for more elaborate cakes and gâteaux. For best results, cream together the fat and sugar really thoroughly before adding the remaining ingredients.

Once baked, creamed cakes will store well in the freezer. If you do not intend to freeze them, they will keep for several days stored in an airtight container.

175g/6oz butter or margarine, softened

175g/6oz caster sugar

3 eggs, lightly beaten

175g/6oz self-raising flour

jam, for sandwiching

icing sugar, for dusting

❶ Preheat the oven to 180C/350F/Gas 4. Grease two 18cm/7 in sandwich tins with a little melted butter or margarine. Line the base of the tins with greaseproof paper and brush the paper with butter.

❷ Place the butter or margarine and sugar in a bowl. Cream with an electric whisk or a wooden spoon until pale and fluffy. (The mixture should easily fall from the spoon if tapped against the bowl.)

❸ Gradually beat in the eggs, a little at a time, using a wooden spoon and beating well between each addition. A tablespoon of flour can be added at this stage to prevent the mixture from curdling.

❹ Sift the remaining flour and add to the bowl. Using a tablespoon or a rubber spatula, gently stir the flour into the mixture until it is just combined. (If it's very stiff, add a tablespoon of milk.)

❺ Turn the mixture into the prepared tins and spread evenly. Bake for 20–25 minutes until risen, golden and just firm to the touch. Turn out on to a wire rack to cool. Sandwich with jam and dust with icing sugar.

From left: Basic creamed cake, Apple and walnut cake and Cherry and almond loaf (recipes overleaf)

Apple and walnut cake

Serves 10
1 quantity Basic creamed cake mixture (see previous page)
50g/2oz walnuts, roughly chopped
2 large cooking apples
demerara sugar, for sprinkling

❶ Preheat oven to 180C/350F/ Gas 4. Grease and base-line a 20–23cm/8–9in round, loose-based cake tin, using well-greased greaseproof paper.
❷ Make one quantity of the Basic creamed cake mixture but fold in all but 2 tablespoons of the chopped walnuts with the flour at the final stage.
❸ Spoon into the prepared tin. Peel, core and slice the apples and arrange them, overlapping them in circles, on top of the cake mixture. Sprinkle cake with the reserved walnuts and the demerara sugar.
❹ Bake in the oven for about 45 minutes until cooked, then remove from the tin. Sprinkle the top of the cake with extra sugar and cool on a wire rack.

Cherry and almond loaf

Serves 10
100g/4oz ground almonds
75g/3oz caster sugar
2 tbsp beaten egg
1 quantity Basic creamed cake mixture (see previous page)
2 tbsp milk
200g/7oz glacé cherries, washed and halved
25g/1oz angelica, finely chopped
100g/4oz icing sugar
almonds and glacé cherries, to decorate

❶ Preheat the oven 170C/325F/ Gas 3. Grease and line a 1kg/2lb loaf tin with well-greased greaseproof paper.
❷ Mix 75g/3oz of the almonds with the sugar and the egg to form a thick paste.
❸ To the Basic creamed cake mixture add the milk, the remaining almonds and the cherries and angelica.
❹ Spoon one third of this mixture into the tin. Press out the almond paste to two rectangles the size of the tin. Place one on top of the mixture. Repeat this with half the remaining cake mixture, then the almond, finishing up with cake mixture.
❺ Bake for 1–1¼ hours. If the top browns too much, cover with foil. Cool.
❻ Mix icing sugar with just enough water to give a thin pouring consistency. Pour over cake and dot with almonds and cherries.

Coffee marble cake

Serves 8–10
175g/6oz sunflower margarine
175g/6oz caster sugar
3 eggs
175g/6oz self raising flour
1 tsp baking powder
2 tbsp instant coffee powder
2 tbsp icing sugar

❶ Pre-heat oven to 170C/325F/ Gas 3. Grease and flour a 25cm/10in ring mould.
❷ Place margarine, sugar, eggs, flour and baking powder in a bowl and beat for 1–2 minutes with a wooden spoon until smooth. Divide mixture in half.
❸ Dissolve 1 tbsp coffee in 1 tsp hot water and stir in to half of the cake mixture. Spoon mixtures alternately into the tin and swirl with a skewer. Bake for 40 minutes until firm.
❹ Sift remaining coffee and icing sugar over cake.

Right: Coffee marble cake

Cheese apricot sandwich

Serves 8

Preheat oven to 170C/325F/Gas 3. Make the Basic creamed cake mixture (see page 141) and add 100g/4oz of chopped ready-to-eat dried apricots. Turn into two greased and lined 18cm/7in sandwich tins. Bake for about 25 minutes until just firm. Cool on a wire rack. Beat together 225g/8oz of cream cheese, $\frac{1}{2}$ teaspoon of vanilla essence and 25g/1oz of icing sugar. Spread over one cake. Top with more chopped apricots and glaze with 2 tablespoons of melted apricot jam. Top with the second cake and dust with icing sugar.

Tangy lemon cake

Serves 8

Preheat oven to 170C/325F/Gas 3. Make the Basic creamed cake mixture (see page 141), adding the finely grated rind of two lemons. Spoon into a deep, greased and lined 18cm/7in round cake tin and bake for about 55 minutes until just firm. Squeeze the juice from three lemons and mix with 40g/1$\frac{1}{2}$oz of caster sugar. Spoon this syrup over the top of the cake while it is still warm for a really delicious tang.

Wholemeal nut loaf

Serves 8

Preheat oven to 170C/325F/Gas 3. Make the Basic creamed cake mixture (see page 141), but substitute wholemeal self-raising flour for white. Stir in 100g/4oz of chopped brazil nuts, 25g/1oz of chopped stem ginger and the grated rind of one orange. Turn into a greased and lined 1kg/2lb loaf tin and bake for about 50 minutes. Cool on a wire rack. Mix 175g/6oz of icing sugar with the juice of one orange and enough water to make a thick paste. Spread this icing over the top.

Country fruit cake

Serves 8 Quick & Tasty

Preheat oven to 170C/325F/Gas 3. Make the Basic creamed cake mixture (see page 141), but substitute soft light brown sugar for the caster sugar and add 50g/2oz of plain flour. Then add 175g/6oz of mixed dried fruit and 50g/2oz of chopped glacé cherries. Spoon into a greased and lined 18cm/7in round cake tin and bake for about 55 minutes until just firm. Remove from tin and cool on a wire rack. Sprinkle top with demerara sugar.

Carrot and walnut cake

Serves 8 Quick & Tasty

Preheat oven to 180C/350F/Gas 4. Grease and line a 22cm/8in round cake tin. Make the Basic creamed mixture (see page 141) and add 100g/4oz chopped walnuts, 225g/8oz grated carrots, and ½ teaspoon ground cinnamon. Spoon into tin and bake for 1 hour or until firm. Beat together 75g/3oz full-fat soft cheese, 50g/2oz butter, a drop of vanilla essence and 100g/4oz icing sugar. Swirl over top and sides of cake and decorate with walnut halves.

Banana and date loaf

Serves 8 Quick & Tasty

Preheat oven to 180C/350F/Gas 4. Grease and line a 1kg/2lb loaf tin. Peel and mash 500g/1lb bananas. Place in a bowl with 100g/4oz sunflower margarine, 75g/3oz muscovado sugar, 2 eggs, 225g/8oz wholemeal flour, 2 tsp baking powder and 100g/4oz chopped dried dates. Beat for 1–2 minutes with a wooden spoon, until smooth. Bake for 1–1¼ hours or until firm.

From left: Cheese and apricot sandwich and Wholemeal nut loaf

MELTED CAKES

Melted fat with sugar or syrup beaten into dry ingredients creates a melted mixture.

Spicy syrup cake

Serves 9

100g/4oz butter or margarine
225g/8oz golden syrup
225g/8oz plain flour
1 tsp ground mixed spice
1 tsp bicarbonate of soda
150ml/¼ pint milk
2 eggs, lightly beaten
25g/1oz caster sugar

❸ Stir the milk into the melted mixture. Add the two eggs and caster sugar to the dry ingredients, then gradually pour the melted mixture into the bowl, stirring very carefully with a wooden spoon.

❶ Preheat oven to 160C/325F/ Gas 3. Grease an 18–20cm/7–8in square tin. Line the base and sides with greaseproof paper and grease again.

❹ Beat thoroughly (still using the wooden spoon) to smooth out lumps. You can throw in some chopped glacé cherries or dried fruit at this stage.

❷ Place the butter or margarine and syrup in a small pan and heat gently until just melted. Sift the plain flour, mixed spice and bicarbonate of soda into a medium-sized mixing bowl.

❺ Pour the mixture into the tin. Bake in the centre of the oven for 50–60 minutes until firm and a skewer inserted into the cake comes out clean. Transfer to a rack to cool.

Sticky gingerbread

Serves 12

1 quantity Spicy syrup cake mixture (see left), using
175g/6oz black treacle and only 50g/2oz golden syrup
2 tsp ground ginger
8 pieces stem ginger, thinly sliced
25g/1oz angelica, cut into sticks
glacé icing, made from 100g/4oz icing sugar, to decorate

❶ Grease and line a 1kg/2lb loaf tin. Prepare the basic melted mixture by following the steps 1–3,

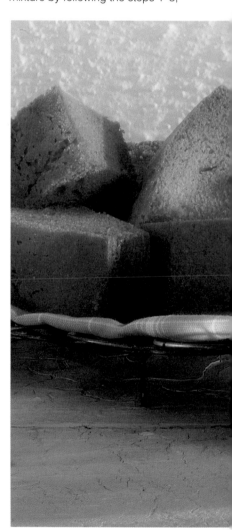

left, but substitute the treacle for some of the golden syrup and add the ground ginger. Pour mixture into the loaf tin and bake, as indicated in step 5 below left.

❷ Transfer the cake to a wire rack and leave to cool. Carefully arrange the stem ginger and sticks of angelica in the centre of the cooled cake.

❸ To make the glacé icing, mix the icing sugar with enough water to give it a thin, pouring consistency.

❹ Pour the glacé icing into a small piping bag and drizzle it over the top of the gingerbread to decorate.

Courgette loaf

Serves 12

225g/8oz courgettes

1 quantity Spicy syrup cake mixture (see page 146), substituting 6 tbsp sunflower oil for the butter, and reducing the quantity of milk to 3 tbsp

50g/2oz sultanas, roughly chopped

demerara sugar, to dust

❶ Grease and line a 1kg/2lb loaf tin with greased greaseproof paper. Finely grate the courgettes and squeeze dry.

❷ Preheat oven to 160C/325F/ Gas 3. Prepare the basic melted mixture by following the steps left, but replace the butter with the sunflower oil and use the reduced quantity of milk. Add the courgettes and sultanas to the cake mixture, as in step 4 left.

❸ Spoon the mixture into the loaf tin and bake for about 1 hour 10 minutes. Sprinkle with demerara sugar and leave to cool in the tin for about 10 minutes. Transfer to a wire rack to cool completely.

From left: Spicy syrup cake and Sticky gingerbread

Glazed fruit gâteau

Serves 12

50g/2oz unsalted butter

4-egg quantity Whisked cake mixture ie 4 eggs, 4oz plain flour, 4oz sugar (see page 149)

600ml/1 pint double cream

2 tbsp icing sugar

4 tbsp orange-flavoured liqueur

450g/1lb mixed peaches and apricots

4 tbsp apricot jam

❶ Grease and base-line a 20cm/8in round cake tin with greased greaseproof paper. Heat the butter until just melted and leave to cool slightly.

❷ Prepare the basic mixture following Whisked cake steps 1, 2 and 3. Carefully fold in half of the sifted flour.

❸ Pour the melted butter in a thin stream down the side of the bowl and then fold in with remaining flour until just combined.

❹ Spoon into the tin and bake for about 25 minutes. Cool on a wire rack, then cut the cake in half horizontally.

❺ Whip the cream with the icing sugar and liqueur until it just holds its shape. Use a little to sandwich together the cakes, then place on a plate.

❻ Using a palette knife, spread remaining cream over top and sides of cake to decorate.

❼ Arrange sliced fruit on top. Melt jam with 1 tablespoon of water and use to glaze the fruit. Chill until ready to serve. As this cake is best made on the day that it's eaten, arrange and glaze the fruit as near to serving as possible.

Swiss roll with jam and cream

Serves 8–10

3-egg quantity Whisked cake mixture (see page 149)

caster sugar, to dust

300ml/$\frac{1}{2}$ pint double cream

6 tbsp strawberry or raspberry jam

❶ Preheat the oven to 190C/375F/ Gas 5. Grease and line a 30cm/ 12in × 20cm/8in Swiss roll tin with greased greaseproof paper.

❷ Make the basic mixture (see right) and pour into tin. Bake for about 10 minutes.

❸ Sprinkle caster sugar over a clean sheet of greaseproof paper and invert the cake on to it. Peel off baking paper.

4 Trim off the crisp edges from the cake, then roll up from a short end with the paper. Leave to cool.
5 Whip cream until peaking. Unroll the cake and remove paper, spread on the jam, and then the cream. Roll up, place on a plate with the join underneath. Dust the top of the Swiss roll with caster sugar. Best served fresh but can be kept for 1–2 days in an airtight container.

From left: Swiss roll with jam and cream and Glazed fruit gâteau

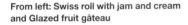

WHISKED CAKES

Whisked sponges contain no fat, so they should be baked at once, and they do not store well unless frozen.

Serves 8
3 eggs
75g/3oz caster sugar
75g/3oz plain flour
raspberry jam
250g/9oz packet ready-to-roll icing
100g/4oz fresh raspberries
icing sugar, to dust

3 Continue to whisk the mixture away from the heat until it is very thick and the whisk leaves a definite trail when it is lifted from the bowl. Sift the plain flour two times onto a sheet of greaseproof paper.

1 Preheat oven to 190C/375F/Gas 5. Grease and line two 18cm/7in sandwich tins. Place eggs and sugar in a large, bowl resting over pan of hot water.

2 Using an electric whisk, beat the eggs and sugar for about 5 minutes until the mixture is pale and foamy (by hand takes longer). Remove bowl from heat.

4 Sift flour into bowl. Fold in flour until it is just combined with egg mixture. Turn into tins and spread carefully. Bake near top of oven for 10–15 minutes.

5 When ready, the cakes should spring back if lightly pressed. Leave to cool, then sandwich with jam. Roll out icing and cover cake. Scatter with fruit and icing sugar.

Chocolate

Cooking with chocolate can be as rewarding as eating it. The luxurious, velvety texture and rich flavour, make chocolate the ultimate treat, and there are few of us who can resist it.

Chocolate apricot tart

Serves 6

175g/6oz plain flour, sifted

2 tbsp cocoa, sifted

2 tbsp caster sugar plus 50g/2oz caster sugar

100g/4oz unsalted butter

2 eggs

150ml/$\frac{1}{4}$ pint milk

150ml/$\frac{1}{4}$ pint single cream

100g/4oz plain chocolate

425g/15oz can apricot halves, drained

150g/5oz canned apricot pie filling

❶ Mix together the flour, cocoa and 2 tablespoons of sugar, then rub in the butter until mixture resembles breadcrumbs. Stir in enough cold water to form a firm dough. Wrap and chill for 30 minutes.

❷ Mix the eggs and remaining sugar. Heat the milk, cream and chocolate until melted then bring to the boil. Pour on to the egg mixture, stirring all the time. Return to the pan and heat gently, stirring constantly until the custard coats the back of the spoon. Cool.

❸ Preheat the oven to 180C/350F/Gas 4. Roll out the pastry and line a greased 20cm/8in loose-bottomed flan tin. Spoon in the custard and top with apricot halves and pie filling.

❹ Roll out pastry trimmings, then cut into twelve 1cm/$\frac{1}{2}$in strips with a pastry wheel and form a lattice across the flan.

❺ Bake for 50–60 minutes until pastry is crisp. Cover with paper if over-browning.

From left: Chocolate apricot tart, Chocolate ice cream with strawberries dipped in chocolate and Chocolate bavarois (recipes overleaf)

PUDDINGS

Chocolate bavarois

Serves 4

2 eggs, separated
50g/2oz caster sugar
175ml/6fl oz milk
25g/1oz milk chocolate
200g/7oz plain chocolate
2 tsp gelatine
90ml/3fl oz double cream,
whipped
150ml/¼ pint double cream
1 tbsp apricot jam, sieved
1 tbsp raspberry jam, sieved

❶ Mix the egg yolks with 25g/1oz of the caster sugar in a large mixing bowl. Put the milk in a small pan and bring slowly to the boil, then pour over the egg mixture, stirring thoroughly with a wooden spoon.

❷ Return the mixture to the pan and stir over a gentle heat until the custard thickens. Add one third to the milk chocolate and the rest to 50g/2oz of the plain chocolate. Stir until the chocolate has melted.

Chocolate ice cream

Try white chocolate instead of plain, and serve ice cream with chocolate-dipped strawberries. Dip them diagonally in melted white chocolate, leave to dry, then dip the other way in plain.

Makes about 1 litre/1¾ pints

2 eggs
2 egg yolks
75g/3oz caster sugar
300ml/½ pint single cream
225g/8oz plain chocolate
300ml/½ pint double cream,
whipped

❶ Whisk together the eggs, egg yolks and sugar in a large bowl. Heat the single cream and chocolate in a small pan until melted and then bring to the boil. Pour on to the egg mixture and stir well.
❷ Return to the pan and heat gently, stirring all the time until the custard coats the back of the spoon. Strain into a bowl, cover the surface of the custard with damp greaseproof paper. Cool.

❸ Fold the whipped cream into the custard and pour into a rigid polythene container. Seal and freeze for 2 hours. Remove from the freezer, whisk well until completely smooth again and then return to the freezer until the ice cream is firm. Before serving, allow to soften in fridge for 20 minutes.

Chocolate and almond cheesecake

Serves 6–8

100g/4oz plain chocolate
500ml/18fl oz single cream
500ml/18fl oz fromage frais
100g/4oz ground almonds
350g/12oz macaroons
120g/4½oz butter
grated chocolate, to decorate

❶ Melt chocolate in a bowl over a pan of hot water. Mix cream and fromage frais in a large bowl. While the chocolate is still warm, pour it into the cream and fromage frais, stirring as you pour – the chocolate should solidify into chips. Stir in almonds.

❷ Pour the mixture into a shallow freezer container and freeze for 3 hours, stirring every 30 minutes.
❸ Put the macaroons in a food processor and reduce to crumbs. Melt the butter and stir into the crumbs. Press mixture over the base and sides of a deep 23cm/9in loose-bottomed flan tin. Chill.
❹ Spoon the fromage frais ice cream into the macaroon case and return to the freezer until just firm. To serve, remove the cheesecake from the flan tin and edge with grated chocolate. Return to freezer and remove 1 hour before serving.

❸ Add the gelatine to two tablespoons of water and leave to swell. Stir one third into the hot milk chocolate custard and the rest into the plain. Whisk the egg whites until stiff and whisk in remaining sugar.

❹ Fold one third of the egg whites and one third of the whipped cream into the milk chocolate and fold the rest into the plain. Divide the milk chocolate mixture among four moulds and chill for 10 minutes.

❺ Add plain chocolate mixture to moulds and chill to set. Melt the remaining plain chocolate in a pan with the cream. Spoon the sauce onto serving plates, drizzle with the jams and turn out set moulds on top.

Chocolate custards

Serves 6–8
300ml/½ pint milk
300ml/½ pint double cream
175g/6oz plain chocolate
4 egg yolks
50g/2oz golden caster sugar
1 tsp cornflour
1 tsp cocoa

❶ Heat the milk and cream in a pan. Add broken chocolate and stir frequently until the chocolate has melted.
❷ Whisk together the egg yolks, sugar, cornflour and cocoa. Add melted chocolate and stir well. Return to the pan and cook over a gentle heat until thick enough to coat the back of a wooden spoon. Test the thickness with your finger.
❸ Serve warm or cold in glasses or Chocolate cases (see right). For a white custard replace plain chocolate with white; and omit cocoa.

Chocolate cases

These stylish chocolate cases are remarkably easy to make. Use them for a special dinner party.

Makes 4
225g/8oz plain chocolate, melted

❶ For each case, cut a double thickness 15cm/6in square of foil. Wrap the foil around a small orange. Pack the foil tightly around the orange, but let the edges and corners remain loose to give a cup shape. Remove orange and press foil case gently on a surface to make a flat base.
❷ Spoon all but 2 tablespoons of the chocolate into foil cases. Smooth up the sides with the back of a spoon.
❸ Place the reserved melted chocolate in a greaseproof piping bag. Snip a small hole at the end and pipe a lacy chocolate edge around the top of each case.
❹ Chill or freeze the cases until set hard, then gently peel away foil, starting around the top edge and gradually working down to base.

Chocolate meringues

Makes 25
1 egg white
50g/2oz caster sugar
1 tbsp cocoa, sifted
100g/4oz plain chocolate
150ml/¼ pint double cream, whipped

❶ Preheat the oven to 120C/250F/Gas ½ and line two medium-sized baking sheets with non-stick baking paper.
❷ Whisk the egg white until stiff, then whisk in half of the sugar. Carefully fold in the remaining sugar and cocoa. Spoon into a piping bag fitted with a 5mm/ ¼in plain nozzle. Pipe fifty 2.5cm/ 1in long spirals well apart on the baking sheets. Bake for 1 hour until crisp and dry. Cool on a wire rack.
❸ Melt the chocolate in a bowl over hot water and dip the meringues diagonally into the chocolate. Leave to set on a wire rack. Sandwich the meringues together with cream and serve at once.

CAKES AND GÂTEAUX

Rich chocolate cake

For baking or decoration, always use a good-quality dessert chocolate or cooking chocolate (*couverture*). The flavour and texture of chocolate cake covering simply don't compare.

Serves 12–15

250ml/8fl oz milk

1 tbsp wine vinegar

350g/12oz plain chocolate

300g/11oz self-raising flour

15g/½oz cocoa

1 tsp bicarbonate of soda

100g/4oz soft margarine

225g/8oz golden caster sugar

2 eggs

225g/8oz ready-to-eat dried apricots

150ml/¼ pint orange juice

450ml/¾ pint double cream

❶ Preheat the oven to 160C/ 325F/Gas 3. Grease and line a 20cm/8in round cake tin. Mix milk and vinegar. Melt 100g/4oz chocolate. Sift flour, cocoa and soda into a bowl. Add margarine, sugar, eggs and half of the milk mixture and beat well.

❷ Add the melted chocolate and the remaining milk; beat until smooth. Spoon into the tin and bake for 1½ hours, or until a skewer comes out clean from the centre. Cool the cake, then split in half.

Folds and flowers gâteau

Serves 12–15

100g/4oz raisins

1 tsp ground cinnamon

50g/2oz walnuts, chopped

1 quantity Rich chocolate cake mixture (see steps 1 and 2 above)

FOR THE DECORATION

100g/4oz butter, softened

200g/7oz icing sugar

25g/1oz cocoa

double quantity plain chocolate Modelling paste (see page 158)

1 quantity milk chocolate Modelling paste (see page 158)

3 white lilies (see page 158)

❶ Stir the raisins, cinnamon and walnuts into the Rich chocolate cake mixture (see above) and bake in a 23cm/9in round cake tin. Cool and place on a plate.

❷ Beat butter, icing sugar and cocoa with one tablespoon of boiling water until smooth. Spread over top and sides of cake.

❸ Take small pieces of plain chocolate Modelling paste, about the size of whole walnuts, and roll out as thinly as possible. Attach around side of cake, letting each piece fall in deep folds.

❹ Continue covering sides then do top of cake. Make ribbons and leaves from milk chocolate Modelling paste (see page 158–9) and use to decorate top along with lilies. Keep in a cool place.

Chocolate cheesecake slices

Makes 12

2 eggs

75g/3oz golden caster sugar

15g/½oz plain flour

15g/½oz cocoa

1 tsp powdered gelatine

225g/8oz white chocolate, melted

450g/1lb curd cheese

200g/7oz Greek strained yogurt

25g/1oz plain chocolate, melted

❶ Preheat the oven to 190C/ 375F/Gas 5. Grease and line an 18cm/7in square, loose-based cake tin.

❷ Beat one of the eggs and 25g/1oz sugar in a bowl over a pan of hot water until the whisk leaves a trail. Sift together flour and cocoa and fold into mixture. Spoon into tin and level surface. Bake for 8–10 minutes until just firm. Turn out cake and leave to cool.

❸ Re-line tin with greaseproof paper. Replace cooled cake.

❹ Sprinkle gelatine over 5 tablespoons of water in a small pan. Beat together the remaining egg, sugar, melted white chocolate, curd cheese and yogurt. Heat the gelatine to melt it, then pour into cheese mixture, beating well. Reserve 1 tablespoon, spread remainder over the cake base.

❺ Beat reserved mixture with plain chocolate. Place in piping bag with writer nozzle. Pipe over cake. Chill and slice.

From left clockwise: Folds and flowers gâteau, Rich chocolate cake and Chocolate cheesecake slices

❸ Roughly chop the apricots. Simmer in the orange juice until soft. Leave to cool, then spread over bottom half of cake. Whip 150ml/$\frac{1}{4}$ pint of cream and spread over apricots. Cover with top of the cake.

❹ Melt the remaining chocolate. Heat the remaining cream until hand hot. Pour cream over the chocolate, whisking well. Chill until thickened, beating several times until the mixture holds its shape.

❺ Spread chocolate cream evenly over top and sides of cake. With a palette knife, smooth from the centre of the cake and down the sides to give a striped finish or swirl with back of spoon and top with chocolate curls. Keep in a cool place, or chill.

MOUSSES

Marbled chocolate mousse

The French word *mousse* literally means 'froth'. Whip the egg whites until they are the same consistency as the chocolate.

Serves 4
100g/4oz plain chocolate
4 tbsp brandy
50g/2oz unsalted butter
100g/4oz white chocolate
2 eggs, separated
150ml/¼ pint double cream

❶ Break up plain chocolate and place with half of the brandy and half the butter in a bowl over simmering water. Turn off heat and leave until melted. Repeat with white chocolate, remaining brandy and butter.

❷ Stir one egg yolk into each bowl of mixture. Place the whites in a clean, grease-free bowl and whisk until they are stiff. Whip the double cream in a separate bowl until it is lightly peaking.

Mini chocolate éclairs

Makes 50
50g/2oz butter
65g/2½oz plain flour, sifted
2 eggs, beaten
150ml/¼ pint double cream, whipped
100g/4oz plain chocolate

❶ Preheat the oven to 200C/ 400F/Gas 6 and moisten two baking sheets with a little cold water.
❷ Melt the butter with 150ml/¼ pint of water in a small pan. Bring to the boil. Add the flour and beat until the mixture forms a ball. Cool slightly, then beat in the eggs a little at a time.
❸ Spoon the mixture into a piping bag fitted with a plain 5mm/¼in nozzle. Pipe fifty 2.5cm/1in éclairs onto baking sheets and bake for 15–20 minutes until they are golden and crisp.
❹ Make a slit in the side of each éclair and leave to cool on a wire rack. Using a palette knife, carefully fill each little éclair with the whipped double cream.

❺ Melt the plain chocolate in a bowl over hot water and dip the top of each éclair in chocolate. Leave them to set in the fridge until ready for serving. Eclairs can be stored, unfilled, in an airtight container, or frozen for one month. Re-crisp in oven before filling.

Layered mousse gâteau

Serves 12
175g/6oz bourbon biscuits
225g/8oz unsalted butter
225g/8oz milk chocolate
6 tbsp brandy or rum
3 eggs, separated
300ml/½ pint double cream
225g/8oz white chocolate
225g/8oz plain chocolate
cocoa and icing sugar, for dusting

❶ Line the sides of a 20cm/8in round, loose-based cake tin with a strip of foil. Finely crush the bourbon biscuits in a polythene bag using a rolling pin. Melt 50g/2oz butter and mix with the crushed biscuits. Press into the base of the tin.
❷ Use the milk chocolate, 50g/2oz butter, 2 tablespoons of the brandy or rum, one egg and 100ml/3½fl oz double cream to make a mousse, following the recipe steps above. Spoon the mousse over the top of the biscuit base. Level the surface and chill thoroughly.
❸ Use the white chocolate, 50g/2oz butter, 2 tablespoons of the brandy or rum, one egg and 100ml/3½fl oz cream to make a white mousse and then use the remaining ingredients to make a dark mousse in the same way. Spoon each layer carefully into the tin and chill well between layers. Finally, chill the completed gâteau overnight.
❹ Dust the surface with cocoa and icing sugar. Remove sides of cake tin and carefully peel away the foil to serve.

Right: Layered mousse gâteau

3 Divide the whipped cream between the chocolate mixtures and carefully fold in, using a metal spoon. Divide the egg whites between the two bowls and fold in gently, taking care to keep in all the air.

4 Place a teaspoonful of dark mousse in each serving glass. Fill with alternating spoonfuls of light and dark mousse. Tap the glasses gently on the surface to get rid of any air pockets as you go.

5 To marble the mousses, push a long, fine-handled teaspoon into each glass. With the tip of the spoon touching the inside of the glass, gently swirl mousses together to achieve a marbled finish. Chill.

Modelling paste

By mixing melted chocolate with syrup or liquid glucose, you can make a highly versatile modelling paste, which is perfect for shaping flowers, leaves, ribbons or other novelty decorations.

Makes 100g/4oz

100g/4oz plain, milk or white chocolate

2 tbsp liquid glucose or golden syrup

❶ Break up the chocolate of your choice and melt in a bowl set over a pan of barely simmering water. Beat in the liquid glucose or golden syrup until the mixture forms a thickish paste which is firm enough to hold together and leave the sides of the bowl clean.
❷ Place in a polythene bag and chill for about 1 hour until set firm.
❸ To use the modelling paste, cut off small pieces and knead lightly in your hands until the paste has warmed up and softened slightly. (If the paste is very firm, it can be softened in a microwave oven for 5–10 seconds.) Roll out, cut and shape as desired. Leftover paste can be kept in a cool place for several weeks and re-used.

Lilies

Mould a piece of foil over thumb, then place upright on a flat surface. Thinly roll out a small amount of white chocolate Modelling paste (see left). For each lily cut out six petals, about 5cm/2in long and 1cm/½in at the widest point. Press the petals,

overlapping slightly around the foil mould. Press together at the top to secure. Chill for 1 hour, then twist the foil mould out of the centre. Press cake-decorating stamens into centre.

Roses

Shape some plain chocolate Modelling paste (see left) into a cone. Press on to surface. Flatten more paste into a petal shape and wrap around cone. Build up petals, making each one larger than the previous one. Once completed, slice off rose just below petals. For buds, used two to three petals and keep them very tightly wrapped around central cone.

Ribbons

Thinly roll out chocolate Modelling paste (see left). Cut into strips. Curl or shape into bows. For marbled ribbon, roughly knead plain and white Modelling paste together. For striped ribbon, lay a thin strip of one colour over another and press down lightly with a rolling pin. For

spotted ribbon, dot a thinly rolled strip with some small pieces of contrasting colour and flatten in with a rolling pin.

Leaves

Thinly roll out chocolate Modelling paste (see page 158) and cut out leaf shapes. Mark veins with the tip of a small knife.

Melting chocolate

Good-quality chocolate used for cases, piping and dipping must be melted correctly for it to work properly. For best results, place the chocolate in a bowl over a pan of hot (but not boiling) water and leave until it has melted and when a temperature of 38–43C/100–110F is reached on a sugar thermometer. If melted chocolate is too cool, it may develop a sugar bloom on setting; or if it is allowed to get too hot, a fat bloom may appear. Chocolate flavoured cake covering is easier to work with but has an inferior flavour.

If you want melted chocolate for ice cream, puddings and cakes, temperature is not crucial. Simply leave the chocolate until it has melted. Alternatively, place in a bowl and microwave on medium powder, allowing 2–3 minutes for each 175–225g/6–8oz. Leave to stand for 5 minutes. Microwave a little longer, if necessary.

Below: These artistic chocolate decorations can be used to enhance your cakes and make them look really professional

Desserts

Sorbets, ice creams, mouth-watering meringues and many other creative dessert ideas. Don't forget to browse through the eggs, batters, pastry and cakes chapters for even more inspiration.

Pavlova

Serves 8

4 egg whites

225g/8oz caster sugar

1 tsp white wine vinegar

2 tsp cornflour

300ml/½ pint double cream

1 peach, sliced

450g/1lb soft fruit (raspberries, black/redcurrants)

2 tbsp Redcurrant jelly (see page 184)

❶ Make meringue (see steps 1–3 overleaf) adding vinegar and cornflour with sugar. Place in piping bag with 1cm/½ in star nozzle.

❷ Mark a 20.5cm/8in circle on parchment, then pipe on mixture working in from edge. Pipe a second circle of meringue on top of the outer edge to form a rim.

❸ Use remaining meringue to pipe decorative border around sides. Bake at 140C/275F/Gas 1 for about 1¼ hours until crisp. Cool.

❹ Whip cream and pipe or spoon into centre. Arrange fruit in centre. Melt jelly and brush over fruit.

Almond meringue layer cake

Serves 8

3 egg whites

175g/6oz light muscovado sugar

100g/4oz toasted almonds, finely chopped

TO DECORATE

50g/2oz ground almonds, toasted

2 tbsp light muscovado sugar

600ml/1 pint double cream, whipped

4 tbsp sherry

❶ Make meringue (see steps 1–3 overleaf), folding in almonds into the mixture. Mark three rectangles 23cm/9in × 10cm/4in on a piece of parchment.

❷ Spoon meringue into rectangles marked, spreading into corners. Bake at 140C/275F/Gas 1 for 1 hour until crisp. Cool. Mix ground almonds with the sugar. Whip cream with sherry.

❸ Place a meringue on a serving plate and spread with some cream. Continue to layer with meringue and the whipped cream. Finally, spread the remaining cream over the top and sides.

❹ Sprinkle the almond mixture over the surface of the meringue and then spread it lightly with a palette knife. Cover the sides in the same way and chill until ready to serve.

From left: Pavlova and Almond meringue layer cake

MERINGUES

Crisp, airy meringue, made simply from egg white, makes a versatile base for various desserts and gâteaux. Sandwich mini meringues with fruit and cream or create a stunning Pavlova. Using brown sugar instead of white gives a richer, more caramelised meringue.

Makes about 16

2 egg whites

100g/4oz caster sugar

❶ Line two baking sheets with parchment. Place egg whites in a thoroughly clean, grease-free bowl and whisk until they stand in stiff peaks.

❷ Sprinkle over a little of the sugar and continue whisking until thoroughly beaten. Continue adding and whisking until two-thirds of the sugar has been added.

Strawberry mousse

Avoid using metal moulds with very acidic fruit as the fruit may react with the metal. Unmould strawberry mousse as soon as it has completely set, or use plastic moulds. Save time on the day by making a mousse the day before and storing overnight in the fridge.

Serves 8

350g/12oz strawberries, hulled

5 tsp gelatine

2 eggs

2 tbsp cornflour

150ml/$\frac{1}{4}$ pint double cream

150ml/$\frac{1}{4}$ pint milk

100g/4oz caster sugar

strawberries, cream and strawberry jam, to decorate

❶ Blend strawberries in a food processor.

❷ Sprinkle gelatine over 3 tablespoons of cold water in a bowl. Leave to soak. Never pour water over gelatine as it sets solid. Always sprinkle over water.

❸ Separate the eggs. Place the whites in a clean, grease-free bowl. Place the yolks in a medium pan with the cornflour. Stir mixture

with a wooden spoon until smooth.

❹ Gradually blend in the double cream, milk and sugar. Bring to the boil, whisking constantly until the mixture becomes smooth and thick. Stir in softened gelatine, then beat in purée.

❺ Whisk egg whites until stiff and fold into mixture. Fold in egg whites and turn into eight individual moulds or one large mould. Chill for several hours. Turn out by

dipping individual moulds in warm water very briefly to loosen, but avoid melting.

❻ To decorate the plates, pipe a fluted border of sieved jam on to a serving plate. Fill the area between the piping and mousse with cream. Decorate with a whole strawberry.

Below: Strawberry mousse

3 Using a metal spoon, gently fold in the remaining caster sugar. The mixture should now be glossy and stiff in appearance ready for the next stage.

4 Fit a large piping bag with a plain or star nozzle, about 1cm/½in diameter. Spoon the meringue mixture into the bag, using a metal spoon.

5 Pipe rounds, about 4cm/2in in diameter, on to prepared baking sheets. Bake at 140C/275F/ Gas 1 or the lowest possible setting for about 1 hour until crisp. Cool.

Fruity ice cream sponge pudding

Serves 6

175g/6oz mixed soft berries, such as redcurrants, blackcurrants and strawberries

juice of ½ lemon

75g/3oz caster sugar

250ml/8fl oz whipping cream

2 × 225g/8oz Madeira cakes

8 tbsp Cointreau

icing sugar, for dusting

extra berries, to decorate

1 Reduce the berries to a rough purée in a food processor, or crush with a wooden spoon. Add the lemon juice and sugar and leave for 2 hours, stirring occasionally, until the sugar has dissolved.

2 Whip the cream until softly peaking and fold into the berry mixture. Pour into a shallow freezer container and freeze for 3 hours, stirring every 30 minutes.

3 Cut the Madeira cakes into 9mm/⅜in thick slices, then cut each slice diagonally to make two triangles.

4 Line the sides of a 1.2 litre/ 2 pint pudding bowl with the sponge triangles, trimming a piece to fit the bottom. Sprinkle over a little of the Cointreau. Spoon in a third of the berry ice cream and cover with a layer of sponge, trim to fit if necessary. Sprinkle over a little more Cointreau, then continue layering the remaining ice cream, sponge and Cointreau, finishing with a layer of sponge.

5 Cover with a double layer of foil and place in the freezer overnight. Remove from the freezer about 1 hour prior to serving, but unmould immediately on to a large dish before transferring it to the fridge. Dust with icing sugar and decorate with berries just before serving.

Yogurt ice cream

Serves 6

225g/8oz granulated sugar

250ml/8fl oz double cream

400g/14oz natural yogurt

1 Place sugar with 250ml/8fl oz water in a heavy-based pan and cook over a low heat, stirring occasionally, until sugar has dissolved. Bring to boil and simmer for 5 minutes. Cool completely.

2 Whip the cream until softly peaking and fold into the yogurt with the cooled sugar syrup. Pour into a shallow freezer container. Freeze, following steps 5 and 6 for Vanilla ice cream (see overleaf).

Ice cream tips

Ice cream and iced desserts come in many guises, from plain old scoops of vanilla to more sophisticated, moulded creations. However – simple or elaborate – the basic recipes are easy, just as the ingredients are straightforward.

Here are a few general points that you should bear in mind.

- The freezer must always be turned to the coldest setting.
- Certain mixtures, usually the less sweet, less rich varieties, need more stirring or beating than others during freezing to achieve the desired smoothness.
- Ingredients must be the best quality. When a flavouring such as an essence is added, its taste will be dulled by freezing, so use a little more than usual.
- Most ice cream needs to be removed to the fridge to soften slowly before serving.
- Although freshly made ice cream can be softened in our recipes, do not soften commercially made ice cream.

See page 165 for our ice bowl recipe for a great serving idea.

Vanilla ice cream

Serves 6

1 vanilla pod or a little vanilla essence (to use essence, see note following recipe)

750ml/1¼ pints milk

6 egg yolks

275g/10oz caster sugar

pinch of salt

❶ Halve the vanilla pod lengthways and place in a pan with the milk. Bring slowly to the boil, then remove from the heat. Leave to infuse for 30 minutes.

❷ Put the egg yolks, sugar and salt in a large bowl and whisk until pale and thick.

❸ Remove vanilla pod from milk, then strain milk on to the egg mixture, stirring constantly. Return mixture to the pan and cook over a low heat, stirring constantly until mixture coats the back of a spoon.

❹ Remove pan from heat, leave to cool, stirring occasionally to stop skin forming.

❺ Pour the mixture into a shallow freezer container. Freeze until the bottom and sides of the mixture are almost firm, then remove from the freezer and beat well with a wooden spoon.

❻ Return the container to the freezer and repeat the freezing and beating process twice to prevent ice crystals forming and to ensure a smooth texture.

- To use vanilla essence: omit step 1 and add warmed milk to egg mixture in step 3 as instructed. Add the essence to taste to the cooled mixture in step 4 and continue with recipe.

Strawberry ice cream

Serves 6

350g/12oz strawberries, hulled

juice of 1 lemon

175g/6oz caster sugar

450ml/¾ pint whipping cream

❶ Place the strawberries in a bowl and crush gently, using a wooden spoon. Or, reduce them to a rough purée in a food processor.

❷ Add the lemon juice and sugar and leave for 2 hours, stirring occasionally, until sugar has dissolved. Whip cream until peaking and fold into the strawberry mixture. Pour into a shallow freezer container and freeze, beating then re-freezing two or three times.

Caramel ice cream with caramel shards

Serves 6

1 quantity Vanilla ice cream (see left)

225g/8oz granulated sugar

FOR THE CARAMEL SHARDS

100g/4oz golden granulated sugar

❶ Put the 225g/8oz golden granulated sugar in a heavy-based pan with 6 tablespoons of water and heat very gently until the sugar has dissolved completely. Raise the heat and boil the sugar until it becomes a rich brown caramel. Cover your hand with a tea towel and carefully pour in 5½ tablespoons water (it will splutter a bit) and stir over a gentle heat until the caramel has dissolved. Leave to cool.

❷ Soften the vanilla ice cream a little and beat in the cold caramel syrup. Spoon the ice cream into six empty yogurt cartons and freeze until firm.

❸ To make the caramel shards: sprinkle the sugar in a thin, even layer on a sheet of lightly oiled foil placed on a baking sheet. Grill until the sugar has melted and caramelised. Leave to cool, then break into irregular pieces.

❹ Dip the ice cream briefly in hot water and invert on to individual plates. Decorate with caramel shards.

Summer fruit ice bowl

sprigs of herbs (eg, mint, lemon balm, feverfew or thyme)
edible flowers (eg, pansies, primulas, violets, rose petals and borage flowers)
seasonal fruits (eg, passion fruit, paw paw, star fruit, plums, nectarines, peaches, strawberries, grapes)

❶ Make the ice bowl first. Half-fill a mixing bowl with cooled, boiled water (boiled water makes a much clearer bowl). Float a slightly smaller bowl inside, then weigh it down (using old-fashioned scale weights or something that can be safely frozen) until the space between the bowls is about 1–2cm/ $\frac{1}{2}$–$\frac{3}{4}$in all round. Secure the bowls together with tape. Fill the space with more water, if necessary.

❷ Push the herbs and flowers into the water, then place on a flat surface in the freezer and leave overnight until thoroughly frozen.

❸ Remove from the freezer and leave for 5 minutes. Remove the inner bowl. Run some cold water over the outside bowl until it can be removed easily. Wrap the ice bowl in foil or polythene and freeze until needed.

❹ When ready to serve, prepare the fruit as necessary and pile into the ice bowl. (Ice cream can also be used to fill the bowl.) Place the bowl on a plate and serve at once. It will last for about 1 hour. Can be frozen for up to 3 months

Below: Ice bowl filled with a variety of ice creams

Lime, passion fruit and tangerine sorbets

Serves 6

pared rind of 3 lemons
200g/7oz granulated sugar
2 tsp powdered gelatine
5 limes
5 tangerines
3 passion fruit
juice of $\frac{1}{2}$ lemon
$\frac{1}{2}$ egg white

❶ Place 750ml/1$\frac{1}{4}$ pints of water, the lemon rind and sugar in a pan. Bring slowly to the boil, making sure that the sugar dissolves completely.

❷ Simmer for 5 minutes, then strain into a jug. Place 3 tablespoons of it in a small, heatproof bowl and sprinkle over the gelatine. Leave to swell, then dissolve over a pan of hot water. Mix into the remaining syrup, then divide among three bowls.

❸ Pare rind from one lime and one tangerine and finely shred. Set aside. Finely grate rind from another lime and add to one of the bowls with juice from two limes. Grate rind from a second tangerine into another bowl with strained juice from two tangerines.

❹ Halve the passion fruit, scoop out pulp. Sieve and add juice to third bowl. Reserve seeds and passion fruit shells to serve it in.

❺ Divide lemon juice into the three mixtures and freeze cooled syrup for 30–40 minutes. Whisk egg white until stiff and divide into three. Fold into each of the fruit syrup mixtures and freeze.

❻ Halve the remaining limes and tangerines and remove the flesh. Scoop frozen sorbets into fruit shells. Return to freezer. Decorate with rind and seeds to serve.

Claret granita

A granita has a wonderful, slushy texture. Ideally it should be eaten the minute it has frozen, so make sure that you start the recipe only a couple of hours before you wish to serve it. This recipe can be made with any wine that you choose.

Serves 6

350g/12oz granulated sugar
300ml/$\frac{1}{2}$ pint claret

❶ Place the sugar in a pan with 300ml/$\frac{1}{2}$ pint of water. Heat gently until the sugar dissolves, then bring the liquid to the boil. Pour in the claret and stir. Allow to cool, then pour into a shallow freezer container and, when completely cold, freeze for 1 hour.

❷ Remove the container from the freezer and stir the mixture to break up the ice crystals. Return to the freezer and repeat the process until you have a mixture of fine-grained frozen crystals and no liquid.

Orange or lemon sorbet

Serves 6

pared rind and juice of 2 oranges
or 3 large lemons
200g/7oz granulated sugar
2 tsp powdered gelatine
$\frac{1}{2}$ egg white

❶ Pour 750ml/1$\frac{1}{4}$ pints of water into a pan and add the orange or lemon rind and sugar. Bring slowly to boil, stirring occasionally to dissolve sugar.

❷ Simmer syrup for 5 minutes. Strain. Place three tablespoons of syrup in a heatproof bowl and sprinkle over gelatine. Leave to swell, then dissolve over a pan of hot water. Strain the orange or

lemon juice and add to syrup with the dissolved gelatine. Leave to cool.

❸ When completely cool, pour the mixture into a shallow freezer container. Freeze for about 30 minutes until it begins to solidify and has turned to a slush.

❹ Whisk the egg white until stiff and fold into the slushy mixture. Return to the freezer and freeze until solid.

Mint and fruit bombe

Serves 6–8

1 quantity Vanilla ice cream (see page 164)

few drops peppermint essence

a little green food colouring

50g/2oz glacé cherries, halved

25g/1oz angelica, chopped

$\frac{1}{2}$ quantity Strawberry ice cream (see page 164)

❶ Divide the vanilla ice cream between two bowls and leave to soften for a few minutes. Add the peppermint essence and green food colouring to one bowl, mixing well to make a pale green colour. Spoon mixture into the base of a 1.5 litre/2$\frac{1}{2}$ pint square mould or cake tin. Place in the freezer until firm.

❷ Stir the glacé cherries and chopped angelica into the remaining bowl of vanilla ice cream. Spoon the mixture on to the peppermint ice cream, spread evenly and return to the freezer until firm. Allow the strawberry ice cream to soften and spread on top of the vanilla in an even layer.

Return the bombe to the freezer until firm.

❸ To unmould the bombe: dip mould briefly in hot water, then run a knife around the edge of the mixture. Place a chilled serving plate on top of the bombe and turn upside down. Carefully lift off the mould. If it still sticks, hold a damp, warm cloth around the tin to help defrost it.

From left: Orange sorbet, Lemon sorbet and Mint and fruit bombe

Amaretti peaches

Serves 4

4 peaches

100g/4oz ground almonds

100g/4oz caster sugar

2 egg whites, lightly beaten

25g/1oz flaked almonds

8 Amaretti biscuits, crushed

❶ Wash the peaches thoroughly. Cut them in half to the stone, twist the two halves and prise out the stone. Set the peaches aside.
❷ Mix together the almonds, sugar and egg whites. Arrange the peaches, cut side up, in a flameproof dish and spoon the almond mixture on top.

❸ Scatter the flaked almonds and crushed Amaretti biscuits over peaches and grill under a lowish heat for 5–10 minutes until the nuts are browned and the peaches are heated through and tender.
❹ Serve peaches at once, accompanied by scoops of Italian ice cream.

Oranges in foil parcels

Serves 4

4 large oranges

4 tsp orange-flavoured liqueur

4 tsp clear honey

1cm/½in piece fresh root ginger, finely grated

25g/1oz butter

❶ Peel the oranges over a bowl using a sharp knife, then cut them into thick wedges. Cut out four large pieces of double thickness foil and place one whole orange on each piece of foil.
❷ Mix the liqueur, honey and ginger into the orange juice that has collected in the bowl, then spoon it over the oranges. Dot the tops of the oranges with butter and fold over the foil to seal them tightly.
❸ Grill for about 15–20 minutes until the fruit is heated through. Carefully open the foil parcels and eat the oranges as they are, or drizzle over some cream, plain fromage frais or Greek-style yogurt.

Left: Amaretti peaches

Brandied clementines with rosemary and ratafia cream

Serves 10

20 clementines
225g/8oz caster sugar
5 tbsp brandy
FOR THE CREAM
6 large sprigs of rosemary
450ml/$\frac{3}{4}$ pint double cream
75g/3oz ratafia or amaretti biscuits, crushed
sprigs of rosemary to decorate

❶ Peel the clementines and prick all over with a fork. Place in a dish.
❷ Place the sugar in a small, heavy-based pan with 3 tablespoons of water. Heat gently, stirring, until the sugar dissolves. Bring to the boil and then boil rapidly until deep golden.
❸ Remove from the heat and add 5 tablespoons water (stand back – it will splutter). Return to the hob and heat gently until smooth. Stir in the brandy and pour it over the clementines. Cool, cover and chill overnight.
❹ To make the cream, place the rosemary and 150ml/$\frac{1}{4}$ pint of the cream in a small pan. Bring to the boil, then cool. Strain, discard the rosemary and chill.
❺ Stir in the remaining cream and whip until peaking. Fold in the biscuits and turn into a serving dish. Decorate the clementines with sprigs of rosemary and serve with the cream.

Right: Vanilla cream with fruits

Vanilla cream with fruits

Serves 10

1 ripe Ogen or Galia melon
2 paw paws (papayas)
100g/4oz blueberries or cranberries
6 tbsp kirsch or orange-flavoured liqueur
4 egg yolks
175g/6oz caster sugar
1 tbsp vanilla essence
450g/1lb mascarpone or light cream cheese
grated rind of 2 lemons
450g/1lb Greek strained yogurt
lemon geranium or mint leaves, to decorate

❶ Halve and remove the seeds from the melon and paw paws and scoop out the flesh using a melon baller or a spoon. Place the flesh in a bowl with the berries and add the kirsch or orange-flavoured liqueur. Set aside.
❷ Whisk the egg yolks and sugar until pale and thickened. Beat in the vanilla essence, cheese and lemon rind until smooth. Stir in the yogurt.
❸ Turn the cream into either one large serving dish or ten individual dessert bowls. Arrange the fruit and liqueur mixture over the vanilla cream and decorate with the lemon geranium or mint leaves. Serve well chilled.

Hazelnut tartlets

Makes 24

225g/8oz plain flour

pinch of salt

100g/4oz butter, diced

75g/3oz hazelnuts

50g/2oz caster sugar

3–4 tbsp milk

450g/1lb mincemeat

grated rind and juice of 1 orange

75g/3oz icing sugar, sifted

❶ Sift the flour and salt into a bowl. Add the butter and rub in until the mixture resembles fine breadcrumbs. Process or finely grind 25g/1oz of the hazelnuts and stir in with the caster sugar. Mix in enough of the milk to make a soft dough.

❷ Knead dough lightly, then wrap in clingfilm and chill in fridge for about 15 minutes. Preheat the oven to 200C/400F/Gas 6.

❸ Chop the remaining hazelnuts and mix into the mincemeat with the grated orange rind and juice.

❹ Roll out pastry thinly and stamp out twenty-four 7.5cm/3in rounds with a fluted cutter. Use to line 24 tartlet tins or sections of bun trays. Prick pastry lightly.

❺ Spoon a little mincemeat into each, then bake for about 15 minutes until the pastry is crisp and brown. Place on a wire rack and allow to cool slightly.

❻ Mix the icing sugar with a little hot water to make a smooth, runny icing. Spoon into a greaseproof paper piping bag, snip the end and pipe zig-zag lines over tartlets. Or drizzle icing from a spoon while they are still warm. Serve with brandy cream.

Christmas trifle

Serves 6

2 eggs

2 egg yolks

2 tbsp cornflour

600ml/1 pint milk

few drops vanilla essence

25g/1oz caster sugar

4 trifle sponges, cut into chunks

6 tbsp orange juice or sweet sherry

1 pomegranate

350g/12oz ripe plums

2 large or 4 small bananas

1 tbsp lemon juice

300ml/$\frac{1}{2}$ pint double cream

❶ Put the eggs, yolks and cornflour into a bowl and whisk the mixture until foamy. Pour the milk into a pan and slowly bring it to boiling point. Then gradually whisk milk into egg mixture until blended.

❷ Return mixture to the pan and cook over a medium heat, stirring continuously, until it has thickened and looks smooth. Stir in the vanilla essence. Take off heat and sprinkle the surface of the custard with the sugar to prevent a skin forming and leave to cool.

❸ Arrange sponges in a glass dish and spoon over the orange juice or sherry.

❹ Halve the pomegranate and scoop out the seeds. Slice plums, discarding stones, and thinly slice bananas. Toss plums and bananas in lemon juice to prevent them going brown. Reserve some of the fruit for decoration and add the remainder to trifle dish.

❺ Pour custard over the fruit and leave to set. Whip cream into soft peaks and spoon over custard, swirling surface with the back of a spoon. Lay reserved fruits on top of the whipped cream and chill until required.

Tiramisu Charlotte

Serves 6–8

150ml/$\frac{1}{4}$ pint espresso or strong black coffee

4 tbsp brandy

32 sponge fingers

icing sugar and cocoa

3 eggs, separated

4 tbsp golden caster sugar

250g/9oz mascarpone cheese

50g/2oz plain chocolate, grated chocolate coffee beans, to decorate

❶ Mix together the coffee and brandy and pour into a shallow dish. Take 16 of the sponge fingers and dip one side briefly in the coffee mixture making sure not to leave them in too long. Press other side of eight sponge fingers in icing sugar, coating them fairly thickly. Press remaining eight sponge fingers in cocoa.

❷ Use the sponge fingers to line an 18cm/7in Charlotte mould or cake tin, placing the dusted sides against the sides of the tin and arranging them alternately. Trim last sponge finger to fit, if necessary.

❸ Beat the egg yolks with the sugar until pale and thickened, then fold in the mascarpone. Whisk the egg whites until stiff and fold them into the mascarpone.

❹ Spoon one third of the mixture into the sponge-lined mould. Dip the remaining sponge fingers into the coffee and brandy mixture and cover the mascarpone cream with a layer of these. Sprinkle the top with a little of the grated chocolate, then add two more layers of mascarpone cream and sponge fingers, finally finishing with a layer of sponge fingers.

❺ Cover the charlotte with a double layer of foil and freeze it overnight. To unmould, dip the charlotte briefly in hot water and invert on to a pretty serving dish. Decorate with the chocolate coffee beans. Return to the freezer and remove 1 hour before you have to serve it.

Left: Hazelnut tarts
Right: Tiramisu Charlotte

Chocolate hazelnut terrine

Serves 6

225g/8oz plain chocolate
1 quantity Vanilla ice cream (see page 164), slightly softened
100g/4oz chopped toasted hazelnuts
150ml/¼ pint double cream, whipped
plain chocolate thins, to decorate

❶ Place the chocolate in a bowl set over a pan of hot water and leave to melt. Place a sheet of greaseproof paper on a work surface and, using a palette knife, spread half of the melted chocolate in a thin layer over the paper. Leave the chocolate to cool and harden.

❷ Place half of the softened vanilla ice cream in a large mixing bowl. Add the remaining melted chocolate and stir thoroughly to combine. Chill.

❸ Line the bottom and sides of a 1.2 litre/2 pint loaf tin with greaseproof paper. Sprinkle base of tin with 3 tablespoons of the chopped hazelnuts and spread over half the remaining softened vanilla ice cream.

❹ Peel the paper away from the hardened chocolate, break chocolate into even-sized pieces and scatter over the vanilla ice cream in the tin. Spread over the chocolate ice cream in an even layer and sprinkle with 6 tablespoons of the chopped hazelnuts. Finish with the remaining vanilla ice cream.

❺ Cover the tin with a double layer of foil and freeze overnight. To unmould, briefly dip the tin in hot water and invert on to a serving dish. Peel off the paper. Decorate the terrine with the whipped cream, chocolate thins and the remaining hazelnuts, and serve in slices.

Yogurt and fruit lollies

Quick & Tasty

Mix equal quantities of natural yogurt and fresh fruit juice or fresh fruit purée; or freeze fruit yogurt or yogurt drinks.

Stew fresh fruit with a little sugar. Cool and freeze in moulds, or simply freeze ready-bought fresh fruit juices.

Milk lollies

600ml/1 pint milk
75g/3oz golden granulated sugar
1 tbsp cornflour

❶ Mix 2 tablespoons of milk with the sugar and cornflour. Heat remaining milk, pour on to cornflour mixture, stir and return to pan. Cook, stirring, until boiling and thickened, then leave to cool. For flavourings, try a few drops of peppermint essence with a little green food colouring, milk shake mix, drinking chocolate, blackcurrant cordial, or fresh orange juice, to taste. Pour into moulds with sticks. Freeze.

Fruit kebabs

Serves 4

4 eating apples, cut into thick wedges and cored
4 bananas, peeled and quartered
4 peaches, quartered and stoned
50g/2oz demerara sugar

❶ Soak eight wooden skewers in hot water for 30 minutes, remove from the water and thread on the fruits alternately. Sprinkle over the sugar and barbecue the kebabs for 5–8 minutes, turning once or twice until the fruits are golden and the sugar has carmelised.

❷ Serve the fruit kebabs hot on their sticks with Greek yogurt or whipped cream – adults can flame the kebabs with a little warmed rum, if they like.

Left: Peppermint, Orange and Chocolate milk lollies

Decorative ideas

Feathered effect

For servings of sorbet, ice-cream and mousses, why not 'feather' the plate. Spread a thin layer of cream over a flat plate. Sieve some jam and place in a piping bag fitted with a plain nozzle. Pipe a spiral over cream, starting at outer edge. Draw a cocktail stick across from centre to edge. Repeat at intervals.

Chocolate leaves

Melt a little plain chocolate and brush thickly over the undersides of some clean small rose or mint leaves. Chill the leaves until they are set, then carefully peel away the real leaves. Use the chocolate leaves as an eye-catching and unusual decoration for chocolate cakes or any fancy gâteaux, mousses and other desserts.

Citrus cases

Cut a slice off the top of an orange. Loosen the edges of the flesh with a sharp-bladed knife, then scoop out using a teaspoon. Pack with sorbet or ice cream and re-freeze until required. Decorate with fruits, mint or lemon balm. Or cut a decorative pattern out of the skin using a groover (canelle knife).

Bed of ice

Put sprigs of mint or small berries in ice-cube trays. Cover with water and freeze. (Alternatively, colour the water pastel pink or green, using a few drops of food colouring.) Turn the ice out into glass bowls. To serve, rest smaller bowls of scooped ice cream or sorbet over the decorative bed of ice.

Sorbet swirls

Sorbets set with gelatine can be partially softened, piped on to plates or trays and re-frozen until they are required. Soften the sorbet at room temperature for about 20 minutes. Then place in a piping bag fitted with a large star nozzle and use to pipe swirls. Pipe the remaining sorbet back into the container.

Mini meringues

Line a baking sheet with non-stick baking paper. Spoon a little meringue into a piping bag fitted with a 3mm/$\frac{1}{8}$in nozzle, or snip the end off a greaseproof bag. Pipe small hearts, butterflies, initials or letters. Bake meringues 140C/275F/Gas 1 for 30 minutes until they are crisp. Store in an airtight tin.

Preserves

Bottle the taste of summer with
these flavoursome, colourful preserves.
Making jams, jellies, chutneys and
pickles has never been so easy.

Sweet barbecue relish

Makes about 2.2.5kg/5lb

1kg/2lb tomatoes

225g/8oz carrots, peeled and diced

1 large onion, peeled and chopped

2 celery sticks, diced

2 green peppers, seeded and diced

150ml/$\frac{1}{4}$ pint white wine vinegar

2 tsp salt

175g/6oz granulated sugar

3 tbsp mustard seeds

1 tsp crushed dried chillies

350g/12oz frozen sweetcorn

❶ Place tomatoes in a large, heatproof bowl. Cover with boiling water and leave for 2 minutes. Peel away tomato skins and roughly chop the flesh.

❷ Put in preserving pan with the other vegetables and vinegar. Simmer until mix is thick but vegetables retain crisp texture.

❸ Add rest of ingredients and continue cooking until thickened, stirring mixture frequently to prevent it sticking to the base of the preserving pan.

❹ Once cooked, the relish should have absorbed all of the liquid but it must not be dry. Spoon relish into cleaned, sterilised jars (see box below).

❺ Label and store for up to six months.

Jar sterilisation

Use ovenproof jars (in 450g/1lb and 900g/2lb sizes) with new rubber seals and spring-clip or screw-band fastenings. Do follow manufacturers' instructions for the use and re-use of preserving jars. The rubber seals will perish slightly after a single heat treatment and should be replaced each time. Jam jars should have plastic-coated lids (not metal ones). Always sterilise before use by washing, drying and placing in preheated oven 150C/300F/Gas 2 for 10 minutes. Fill jars while warm.

Left: Curried fruit chutney
Right: Sweet barbeque relish

Curried fruit chutney

Makes about 1.75kg/4lb

1 tsp crushed, dried chillies

2 tbsp cumin seeds

1 tbsp fennel seeds

15 cardamom pods

1 tbsp ground turmeric

50g/2oz raisins, chopped

2 celery sticks, diced

1kg/2lb cooking apples, peeled and chopped

450g/1lb onions, peeled and chopped

1 small ripe melon, skinned and roughly chopped

300ml/$\frac{1}{2}$ pint distilled malt vinegar

1 tbsp salt

225g/8oz granulated sugar

❶ Sterilise jars, see box, page 175. Place chillies, cumin, fennel and cardamom pods in mortar and crush coarsely with a pestle (or, use a small bowl and the end of a rolling pin). Remove the crushed cardamom pods.

❷ Place spices in a preserving pan with remaining ingredients except salt and sugar. Bring to the boil, reduce heat and simmer until apples have become pulpy.

❸ Add sugar and salt and continue cooking until thickened and most of the liquid has been absorbed. Spoon into warm sterilised jars. Cover and label.

From left: Ploughman's pickle, Provençal pickle and Piccalilli

Ploughman's pickle

Makes about 1.5kg/3$\frac{1}{2}$lb

600ml/1 pint spiced vinegar (see Piccalilli, step 1, right)

225g/8oz each of diced onions, carrots and cucumber

100g/4oz salt

750g/1$\frac{1}{2}$lb tomatoes, skinned and chopped

grated rind and juice of 1 lemon

100g/4oz dates, stoned and chopped

175g/6oz dark muscovado sugar

15g/$\frac{1}{2}$oz cornflour

2 tbsp black treacle

❶ Sterilise jars, see box page 175. Salt onions, carrots and cucumber as explained in Piccalilli, step 2, right. Drain and wash thoroughly.

❷ Place in pan with tomatoes, lemon rind and juice, 450ml/15fl oz of the spiced vinegar, dates and sugar. Simmer the mixture for 10 minutes until all the vegetables are softened.

❸ Mix cornflour with treacle and rest of vinegar. Add to pan. Cook until thickened and most of the liquid has been absorbed. Spoon into warmed sterilised jars, cover and label. Keeps up to six months. Use within four weeks once the pickle is opened.

Provençal pickle

Makes about 1.25kg/2½lb

450ml/15fl oz spiced vinegar, see Piccalilli, step 1, right

1 red, 1 green, 1 yellow and 1 orange pepper

2 large courgettes, sliced

1 onion, sliced into rings

175g/6oz salt

3 garlic cloves, skinned

12 pitted black olives

40g/1½ oz granulated sugar

3 bay leaves and thyme sprigs

100g/4oz cherry tomatoes

❶ Sterilise one large or two small jars, see box, page 175. Seed and finely slice peppers and salt with the courgettes and onion (see Piccalilli, step 2 right). Drain and wash vegetables thoroughly.

❷ Cut garlic cloves lengthways into quarters, and push inside olives. Halve olives crossways.

❸ Place spiced vinegar, sugar and herbs in a pan and heat through until sugar is thoroughly dissolved. Cool.

❹ Layer peppers in base of jars. Cover with a layer of olives, pressing cut sides against the glass and pack courgettes into centre. Then layer onions and tomatoes and repeat to use up vegetables. Pour over vinegar. Cover, label and refrigerate. Use within two weeks.

PICKLES

Piccalilli

Makes about 3kg/7lb

1.2 litres/2 pints spiced vinegar, see step 1 (make in advance)

2.75kg/6lb diced cucumber, onions, French beans, small cauliflower florets

450g/1lb salt

150g/5oz granulated sugar

1 tbsp mustard seeds

15g/½oz ground ginger and turmeric

25g/1oz cornflour

❶ For spiced vinegar: crush 25g/1oz mixture of mustard seeds, peppercorns and allspice. Pour vinegar into jar, add four bay leaves and a cinnamon stick. Leave vinegar for several weeks.

❷ To salt vegetables: layer vegetables in a large colander, sprinkling each layer generously with salt. Leave for 12 hours or overnight. Wash and drain thoroughly.

❸ Tip vegetables into preserving pan. Stir in sugar and all but 75ml/3fl oz of the spiced vinegar and cook gently until the sugar completely dissolves.

❹ Sprinkle spices into pan. Bring to the boil, reduce heat and simmer gently until vegetables are softened but not pulpy. Blend cornflour with remaining vinegar.

❺ Add cornflour, cook until thick. Sterilise jars (see box, page 175). While hot, bottle. Store for four weeks. Keeps one year. Use within four weeks once opened.

BOTTLING

Soft and firm-textured fruit can be bottled, as long as it is just ripe and in perfect condition. Store in a cool, dark place and it will keep well for several months.

Bottled soft fruit

Makes about 1.75kg/4lb

1.75kg/4lb mixed soft fruit, such as strawberries, raspberries, red, black and white currants

225g/8oz granulated sugar

pared rind of 1 lemon

❶ Remove the rubber seals from the lids of the jars and soak in soapy water; rinse. Preheat oven to 150C/300F/Gas 2. Clean jars and sterilise for 10 minutes in the oven. Discard stalks and damaged fruits.

❷ Place sugar and 600ml/1 pint of water in a heavy-based pan and heat gently, stirring occasionally, until the sugar has dissolved. Bring to the boil and cook vigorously for 1 minute until syrupy.

Brandied pears with cinnamon

Makes about 1.75kg/4lb

275g/10oz granulated sugar

2kg/4½lb firm cooking pears

2 cinnamon sticks

50g/2oz blanched almonds

8 tbsp brandy

❶ Clean and sterilise two 900g/2lb jars (see step 1 above). Make a syrup with the sugar and 900ml/1½ pints of water (see step 2 above). Peel, halve and core pears and simmer in the syrup for 10 minutes until soft.

❷ Pack the pears, cinnamon and almonds into the warmed jars. Add brandy to the syrup and pour over pears. Finish as steps 3–5 above, allowing 1 hour cooking time.

Apricots in honey syrup

Makes about 1.75kg/4lb

175g/6oz granulated sugar

50g/2oz clear honey

15g/½oz stem ginger, finely chopped

1.75kg/4lb apricots

❶ Clean and sterilise two 900g/2lb jars (see step 1 above). Make a syrup with the sugar and 600ml/1 pint of water (see step 2 above), then stir in the honey and ginger.

❷ Halve and stone the apricots and pack tightly into jars. Pour over the honey syrup. Finish as steps 3–5 above, cooking for 40 minutes.

Left: Brandied pears with cinnamon

❸ Pack the fruit and lemon rind into the warmed jars. Press down gently until the jars are filled to within 2.5cm/1in of the top. Stand the jars in a roasting tin lined with a few layers of newspaper.

❹ Pour over the syrup to just cover the fruit. Tilt jars to remove air bubbles. Replace the rubber seals and glass lids (do not tighten clips or screw-bands). Cook in centre of oven for 30 minutes.

❺ Remove the jars from the oven and place on a wooden surface (a cold surface could make the glass crack). Replace the spring-clips or screw-bands, screwing the bands as tightly as possible, and leave to cool. When the jars are quite cold, remove the clips or bands and carefully lift each jar by its glass lid – if the lid stays on, the seal is airtight. Store jars without replacing the clips or bands, as repositioning may disturb the seal. (If a lid does come off, eat the fruit as soon as possible.)

Cherries in gin

Makes about 450g/1 lb

Clean and sterilise a 450g/1lb jar (see step 1 above). Prick over 225g/8oz washed cherries with a cocktail stick or skewer and pack into a jar. Add enough sugar to come half way up jar, then pour over about 150ml/$\frac{1}{4}$ pint gin to cover. Add a tight-fitting lid and leave the jar for three days, shaking occasionally, until the sugar has completely dissolved. Store for up to one year. Serve (small portions!) as a dessert with cream or custard. Alternatively, use for drinks, decorating with the cherries. (Use the same method to bottle plums or apricots in other spirits, such as brandy, kirsch or white rum.) Keep out of reach of children!

Right: Cherries in gin

Herb vinegar

Makes ½ pint

Sterilise bottles, see box, page 175. Bruise some fresh herbs, such as tarragon, rosemary or dill, and place in a bowl. Add 300ml/½ pint white, red wine or cider vinegar. Cover and stand for three days. Place a fresh sprig of appropriate herb in a bottle and add drained vinegar, topping up if necessary. (A slice of lemon adds colour and flavour to thyme vinegar.) Seal with a lid or cork and store for up to one year. Use in dressings and sauces.

Soft fruit vinegar

Makes about 750ml/1¼ pint

Sterilise bottles, see box, page 175. Place 450g/1lb strawberries, raspberries and redcurrants in a bowl. Add 600ml/1 pint white wine vinegar. Cover and stand for four days. Strain the vinegar and bottle. Store for up to a year and use in dressings and sauces for meat and game.

Oriental pickled salad

Makes about 1.5kg/3lb

Sterilise jar, see box, page 175. Slice 100g/4oz button mushrooms. Dice ½ an orange. Halve lengthways 100g/4oz baby corn cobs. Layer with 100g/4oz salt (see Piccalilli, step 2, page 177) and leave for 12 hours. Drain. Skin and slice four garlic cloves. Wash and drain 225g/8oz fresh beansprouts and mix with the vegetables, garlic, 2 tablespoons of chopped chives and some star anise. Pack into a 1.5kg/3lb jar. Heat 600ml/1 pint distilled malt vinegar with 175g/6oz granulated sugar, 2 tablespoons of light soy sauce and season with some black pepper. Stir until dissolved. Pour over vegetables. Cover and refrigerate for up to one month. Serve as an accompanying salad.

Feta cheese in garlic and herb oil

Makes about 350g/12oz

Thoroughly wash and dry a 350g/12oz jar. Sterilise in a preheated oven 150C/300F/Gas 2 for 10 minutes. Mix one strip finely chopped red pepper, ½ small, finely chopped onion, chopped fresh herbs, three garlic cloves, peppercorns and 200ml/7fl oz olive oil. Add 200g/7oz diced feta cheese and stir. Spoon into a sterilised jar, top up if necessary. Push a bay leaf down the side of the jar. Store the cheese in the fridge and eat within three weeks.

Left: Feta cheese in garlic and herb oil
Right: A variety of herb vinegars

CORDIALS

Refreshing fruit drinks are a perfect way of using up summer fruit that is either over-ripe or too soft for making into other preserves. Once made, they will keep in the fridge for up to six weeks. Always store in sterilised bottles. Wash and dry bottles thoroughly then place in a preheated oven 150C/300F/ Gas 2 for 10 minutes.

Serve cordials diluted to taste with water or add to sparkling white wine for a more sophisticated drink rather like a *kir* (crème de cassis and dry white wine). Or whisk a tablespoonful of cordial into a glass of fresh, chilled milk. Stir cordial into some plain yogurt, or spoon it over ice cream.

Blackcurrant cordial

Makes about 1.75 litres/3 pints
1.75kg/4lb blackcurrants
grated rind and juice of 2 lemons or 2 limes
granulated sugar (see step 2)

❶ Sterilise bottles, see Cordials, left. Place blackcurrants, rind and juice and 1.2 litres/2 pints of water in a pan. Bring to the boil, stirring and crushing until softened.
❷ Strain fruit pulp through jelly bag, see jellies, overleaf, step 3. Measure juice and return it to the pan but only stir in 350g/12oz sugar for each 600ml/1 pint of juice. Heat gently to dissolve sugar. Pour into sterilised bottles.

Strawberry, raspberry or loganberry cordial

Makes 1.75 litres/ 3 pints

Follow the Blackcurrant cordial recipe (left), substituting the chosen fruit. Do not add any water, though, and follow the method exactly.

Redcurrant cordial

Makes 1.75 litres/ 3 pints

Follow the Blackcurrant cordial recipe (left) but substitute redcurrants instead of blackcurrants.

Blackberry cordial

Makes 1.5 litres/ 2½ pints

Follow the Blackcurrant cordial recipe (left), but reduce the quantity of water to just 300ml/½ pint and follow the method exactly.

Nectarine or peach cordial

Makes 600ml/ 1 pint

Halve, stone and roughly chop six ripe peaches or nectarines. Simmer in a pan with the juice of three oranges and 300ml/½ pint of water. Follow the Blackcurrant cordial recipe (left).

Left: Nectarine and Strawberry cordials
Right: Redcurrant and Blackberry cordials

JELLIES

Jellies can be served like jam or as an accompaniment to meat dishes and can be flavoured with herbs. As only the juice is used, the yield is much lower than that of jam. Always test the pectin level after straining pulp (see below). If you don't have a jelly bag, tie clean muslin to the legs of an upturned stool.

Redcurrant jelly

Makes about 1.5kg/3lb
1.75kg/4lb redcurrants
preserving or granulated sugar

❶ Discard any bruised or damaged fruits (it is not necessary to remove the stalks, as they will be extracted when the pulp is strained). Wash redcurrants, if necessary, and place in a preserving pan.

❷ Add 600ml/1 pint of water to the pan, cover and bring to the boil. Remove the lid and simmer gently for 30 minutes, stirring and mashing the fruit frequently until it becomes very soft and pulpy.

Peach and apple jelly

Makes about 1.25kg/2½lb
6 ripe peaches, quartered
900g/2lb cooking or crab apples, cut into chunks
1 orange, sliced
preserving or granulated sugar
sprigs of mint, thyme, rosemary, sage, oregano or lemon balm

❶ Place fruit, stones and cores in a preserving pan with 300ml/½ pint of water and simmer gently for 30 minutes. Follow Redcurrant jelly steps 3–5 above, but only half fill jars. Add herbs then pour over remainder. Cover and label.

Spiced bramble jelly

Makes about 1.5kg/3lb
1.75kg/4lb blackberries
3 lemons, sliced
1 cinnamon, stick, lightly crushed
1 tbsp whole cloves
preserving or granulated sugar

❶ Place the blackberries and lemon slices in a preserving pan with the cinnamon, cloves and 85ml/3fl oz water.
❷ Simmer for 20 minutes, stirring frequently until berries are tender. Strain through a scalded jelly bag and complete as for Redcurrant jelly, steps 3–5 above.

From left: Peach and apple jelly and Spiced bramble jelly

❸ Scald a jelly bag in boiling water and suspend it over a large bowl. Spoon pulp into bag and leave for at least 4 hours, or until it stops dripping. Don't squeeze bag as jelly will become cloudy. Measure strained juice and weigh 450g/1lb sugar for each 600ml/1 pint.

❹ Warm sugar in preheated oven, 160C/325F/Gas 3, in an ovenproof bowl, then dissolve in the juice. Boil until set is reached. Test by placing a teaspoonful on a cooled saucer. If it wrinkles when pushed, setting point is reached. Remove pan from heat.

❺ Skim scum off with a slotted spoon. Wash and dry jars. Sterilise in oven at 150C/300F/Gas 2 for 10 minutes. Pour jelly into warm jars, cover with waxed paper discs (shiny side down). Dampen cellophane lids, stretch over jars and secure with rubber bands.

Pectin

Pectin is a soluble, gum-like substance in the pips, pith and flesh of most fruit. It gels when heated with sugar and fruit acid, and the set depends on the balance between these ingredients and on the variety of fruit and degree of ripeness.

Test low-pectin fruit, such as strawberries and apricots, by mixing 1 teaspoon of juice with a little methylated spirit. Stir and leave to settle. If it forms a jelly, there is enough pectin; if it remains liquid or forms small balls, more pectin is required. To rectify, add one grated cooking apple for every 900g/2lb fruit.

JAMS

The following recipe can be made with any other fruit that is high in pectin, such as redcurrants, plums, blackcurrants and apples.

Gooseberry jam

Makes about 3kg/7lb

1.75kg/4lb preserving or granulated sugar

1.75kg/4lb gooseberries

grated rind and juice of 2 lemons

10–12 lemon geranium leaves or elderflower heads, chopped

❶ Preheat the oven to 160C/ 325F/Gas 3 and warm the sugar in an ovenproof bowl for 15 minutes. Top and tail the gooseberries, then place in a preserving pan with 300ml/½ pint of water and the lemon rind and juice.

❷ Bring the fruit to the boil, stirring frequently. Reduce the heat and simmer gently for about 20 minutes or until the gooseberries are pulpy. Stir in the chopped geranium leaves or elderflowers.

Strawberry jam

Makes 3kg/7lb

1.75kg/4lb preserving sugar

1.75kg/4lb strawberries

juice of 3 lemons

❶ Put the preserving sugar into an ovenproof bowl and warm at 150C/300F/Gas 2 for 15 minutes. Heat strawberries and lemon juice in a preserving pan for about 5 minutes.

❷ Add warmed sugar and stir over low heat until dissolved. Bring to the boil, skimming off any scum that comes to the top. Boil for 10–15 minutes until the setting point is reached.

❸ To test for a set, place some jam on a saucer and chill in fridge for 2 minutes. Push it with your fingertip; if it wrinkles, the setting point has been reached. If not, boil the mixture again and test again.

❹ Leave to stand for 10 minutes (the fruit may rise to the surface if the jam is bottled immediately).

Left: Strawberry jam

❸ Add the warm sugar and heat gently until dissolved. Bring to the boil and, with a slotted spoon, skim off any scum that rises. Boil for 10–15 minutes until setting point is reached. Remove from heat.

❹ Test for a set by placing a drop of jam on a cold saucer and chill for 2 minutes. If it wrinkles when you push it, setting point has been reached. If it doesn't, boil for a little longer and test again. Leave to stand for 10 minutes.

❺ Meanwhile, wash and dry jars and heat at 150C/300F/Gas 2 for 10 minutes. Ladle jam into jars. Cover immediately with waxed discs, shiny side down, and dampened cellophane lids. Secure with rubber bands. Label and store in a cool, dark place.

Ladle jam into jars which have been washed, dried and sterilised at a temperature of 150C/300F/ Gas 2 for 10 minutes.
❺ Now cover with waxed discs, waxed sides down. Dampen Cellophane lids, then stretch over jars. Secure with rubber bands. Label the jars and store in a cool, dark place for up to one year.

Apricot jam

Makes about 3kg/7lb
1.75kg/4lb fresh apricots
1.75kg/4lb preserving sugar
juice of 2 lemons

❶ Halve and stone the apricots. Crack open apricot stones with a hammer or rolling pin. Set aside kernels and then peel away the skins.
❷ Warm the sugar as in Gooseberry jam, step 1 above.
❸ Heat fruit with kernels, lemon juice and 600ml/1 pint water. Follow Gooseberry jam, steps 3–5 above, testing for setting point after 10 minutes.

Blackberry and apple jam

Makes about 3kg/7lb
1.75kg/4lb preserving sugar
1kg/2lb blackberries
1kg/2lb cooking apples, peeled and chopped
juice of 2 lemons
handful of chopped mint (optional)

❶ Warm the sugar as in Gooseberry jam, step 1 above.
❷ Heat fruit and lemon juice in preserving pan for about 10 minutes. Follow Gooseberry jam, steps 3–5 above, testing for setting point after 10 minutes.

Greengage and lime jam

Makes about 2.75kg/6lb
1.75kg/4lb preserving or granulated sugar
1.75kg/4lb greengages, stoned
grated rind and juice of 4 limes

❶ Warm the sugar, as in Gooseberry jam, step 1 above.
❷ Heat greengages in a preserving pan with lime rind and juice and 300ml/$\frac{1}{2}$ pint of water. Simmer for 15 minutes until pulpy.
❸ Add the sugar and stir until dissolved. Follow Gooseberry jam, steps 3–5 above, testing for a set after 5 minutes.

Index

Page numbers in bold refer to photographs.